CLOOT
AN
SHEEP SH

by

Bunty Cowe.

First published 1995.

ISBN 0 9526496 0 8

British Library Cataloguing–in–Publication Data. A catalogue record for this book is available from the British Library.

Published by F.L. Kennington, Northumbria House, Corbar Road, Stockport SK2 6EP.

Printed by Parchment (Oxford) Ltd., Printworks, Crescent Road, Cowley, Oxford OX4 2PB.

CONTENTS   PAGE.

Dedicated to Mum and Dad
who took me to College Valley

ACKNOWLEDGEMENTS

Special thanks to my husband who has supported me
in preparing this book, not only by his interest in
Northumberland and its history and social history, but
by typing the text and revising it as memories were
recalled. Also to my family, Ann, Colin, Gerry and
Angela for their help.
Sincere thanks also to all those giving encouragement
and information.
To my cousin, Nellie McLain (Mrs.Cock) of East Ord
for memories and many laughs recalling the past.
To Susan Robinson and David Rowbottom for reading
the text.
Mrs.Ann Telfer of Milfield for her advice.
Colin Matheson for loan of the cover photo.
T.W.Reid of Stockport Library.
The staff of Northumberland Record Office and
Library Service for documents and help, and without
whom it would probably never been written.
To all those people from Wooler and district whose
memories have been taxed.
Finally, to the printers, Parchment Press, for their
unfailing help and courtesy.

Front cover: College Valley, with me as a child.

Rear cover: Coldburn 1993, taken by my husband.

INTRODUCTION

Remote in its hollow in the gentle green hills, carpeted – sometimes with wild flowers – sometimes with snow – but always dominated by 'Muckle Cheviot', lies the College Valley.

If you live in north Northumberland, or across in the Eastern Borders of Scotland, you will be familiar with the great hump of Cheviot's 2700 feet, with its little cap of the West Hill Cairn, and the other nearby hills of Hedgehope, Yeavering Bell, etc. You may not be so familiar with the valleys, and you may never have been into the College Valley.

Even if you are not a 'local', you may be one of the thousands of dedicated walkers who traverse the 270 mile length of the Pennine Way from its peaty blackness of Derbyshire's Kinder Scout, not far from my present-day home, to the peat bogs of Cheviot and on to Kirk Yetholm.

They will have looked down from Auchope Rig and been cheered by the sight of College Valley as they plod on down to Yetholm.

This is the place where I spent my formative years and I can look back and remember the pleasure of a childhood spent there.

Now much has been written about the lives of the shepherds, but little or nothing about the lives of the women and children who contributed so much to the community. My childhood there was in the 1930s and a world away from the 1990s, much harder in many ways, but lacking todays materialism. Because of the War, we had to leave the Valley and move to Berwick, where I met and married Fred Kennington. We moved south, eventually coming to Stockport in 1963. But the Valley was never forgotten and we have returned as often as possible.

I have been encouraged to record what I remember – you might like to share some of my memories, too.

But first I have to set the scene............

Margaret Kennington (Bunty Cowe),
Stockport. 1995.

4

IN THE BEGINNING...............

To put the College Valley into place on a map — it lies a few miles west of Wooler and where the College Burn flows north from its source on 'Muckle Cheviot' to join the Bowmont Water at Westnewton to form the River Glen. In turn, the Glen flows into the Till and subsequently into the River Tweed. The name 'College' has nothing to do with education. It is thought to come from Old English, meaning a stream flowing through boggy land.

The valley is private, owned now by the Sir James Knott Trust and apart from walkers for whom there is a right of way, one needs a permit to take a car up the valley road. No cars are allowed at all during lambing time. The countryside is green and partly wooded. Many of the trees are conifers but in 1995, the Trust has removed some of these conifers and is replacing them with indigineous trees. There is also a mass of whin(gorse) in flower in May and June, and a delight to see.
In my time there were not many inhabitants, and now even fewer, far outnumbered by sheep and a few shy wild goats.

Westnewton lies at the foot of the valley. It doesnt seem to have changed much since my days, and I always look at the plants growing in the wall when I pass there. After Westnewton, you go up a steep hill with clear memories of a hard slog on a bike all those years ago! Crab apples grow on the side of the road and we still pick them to make delicious crab apple jelly — something you cant buy in the supermarket. Soon the way descends passing, over on the hill on the left, Hethpool Bell, the stunted oaks planted for Admiral Collingwood to provide oak for his 'wooden walls of England'. Regrettably the climate and the soil did not favour them. On the right is the track leading to Trowburn Farm and the site of former 'shielings' (shepherds cottages) now gone. Through the little wood lies Hethpool and the end of the narrow public road. After that it is a private road with a right of way for walkers.
Now you are in the narrow valley with its stony burn and carpet of yellow whin while the peaty blackness of Cheviot lies ahead.
The field in front I knew as Little Hetha — the place where I picked mushrooms. Strictly speaking, Great Hetha and Little Hetha are the hills on your right, each the site of ancient British Camps, so the

place has been inhabited for a long time. The field I called Little Hetha, if you look carefully, is quite bumpy. I was always told that the humps formed part of ancient British cultivation.

The ideal time for me has always been the whin blossom time, but each season has its own particular beauty. There is the mass of wild flowers in summer; late summer and early autumn bring the heather and then the golden bracken; and in winter there is the snow-clad Cheviot. Even coming back out of the valley there is the feeling of remoteness and enclosure as coming north to Hethpool you face the lump of Hethpool Bell which appears to block your way out.

Having decided to to recount my memories of childhood, I found I had to look a bit further into the history of the area. One of the items I came across was a Catalogue for the sale of the Hethpool and Burton Estates in 1918. Burton is in Northumberland, not near Wooler, but near the coast and a mile or so behind the great Castle at Bamburgh. Co-incidentally, Dad's family had lived there until the 1920s. Both estates were owned by Earl Grey, and the catalogue contains a wonderful piece of the P.R. of the day.

It says 'The College Valley is widely acknowledged to be Queen of the Valleys and a holiday resort for the busy city man. Its attractions cannot be measured in terms of money. The air is bracing and healthful; the scenery imposing, etc...it is one of the recognised roads by which entry was obtained into Northumberland by Scottish raiders'. The Estate was said to be 1294 acres and the rental was £717 per annum. The words must have been appealing as it was bought by the shipowner, Sir Arthur Sutherland.

Returning to lesser mortals, this is where I spent my childhood – a happy one which has influenced my life and given me a love of the country – my North Country. Life was very different then and fifty years on the memories may be a little dimmed, indeed some may not be correct. It may be that somebody will read this and correct them for me.

MY FAMILY....

I was born Margaret Roberta Cowe, but called Bunty by the family, not in the valley, but at Belford Moor Farm, 15 miles away. My father, David William Cowe came from a Northumbrian family

6

which, two generations earlier had come across the Border from Hutton in Berwickshire. There his family had been carters and family legend says they carried stone for the building of Coldstream Bridge. Dad's greatgrandfather went off to Coldstream Toll, the local equivalent of Gretna Green and had an irregular marriage – that was the romantic thing in those days – before returning to Hutton to face the wrath of the 'Kirk'. The entry in the Register for Hutton Church reads 'William Cowe and Mary Learmonth, both of Fishwick Mains were in irregular marriage at Coldstream on 10th August 1822. Rebuked in the Session and the marriage confirmed'. Like Gretna Green, many of the Border Tollhouses were used in this way and it seems to have been the romantic thing to do, at least sometimes!. And it was a good living for the self-styled 'priests' William moved across the Border from Hutton to West Newbiggin, Norham, and his brother moved to Norham, where the family set up a baker's shop.

My grandfather, Robert Cowe, started work as a farmworker, but early in life left to work on the railway at Newcastle. He worked on the big crossover just outside Newcastle Central Station and on retirement in 1923, was Permanent Way Inspector at Tyne Dock.

Dad, too, started on the railway but he did not like it and became an apprentice cabinet maker with Galashons at Newcastle, without parental approval. He got himself a job there, each morning taking his 'bait' and going out at the right time. Only weeks later did his parents find out. He had always wanted to work with wood. At school he always had a penknife and a piece of wood and was often in trouble for whittling away under his desk. He was also left-handed and in those days that was not allowed. He was made to use his right hand for writing by forcing him to hold something in his left hand. So he became ambidextrous! He was totally opposed to anyone being forced to be right-handed if that was not natural. He became a very competent Cabinet Maker, making many items for the house. Some we could not accomodate after his death and they were given to Beamish Museum, where they can be seen and provide a memorial to him. Much later in life, he taught Technical Drawing, etc. in Berwick and many there will remember him. Dad served in the Great War, being badly wounded. He suffered from malaria for much of his life, and coupled with the effects of shellshock, it affected his general health. His wartime injuries did

The family c.1933. From the right, Mum, Dad, Winnie, me.

Us with Vicky, our Border Terrier, Prue,'Ernie Bertram's 'ghost' and the 'stranger' on the right is visitor, Rix Duncan, from Cullercoats.

cause particular problems to the extent that he was advised to move out of Newcastle to a quiet place. Early in the 1920s, Mum and he took a cottage at Glororum, mear Bamburgh, where he set up in business as a Joiner and Cabinet Maker on his own. His work took him all over Northumberland and he was often away from home. I know he fitted a staircase in Callaly Castle and he worked, too, on Holy Island, lodging at the 'Iron Rails'. Since his mother, Margaret Ann Waugh, had lived there with her parents, he was accepted there - an otherwise insular place in the 1920s/1930s.

Mum, Agnes Dent, was born in Newcastle, the daughter of a Yeast and Egg Merchant in Heaton. She spent her childhood in Old Durham, a hamlet east of Durham City, and one with an interesting history. She returned to Heaton, and trained as a Teacher in Newcastle. Due to Dad's wartime illness she left teaching and moved with him to Glororum and later to Belford. As his health improved, she decided to return to teaching and in January 1929 she took the job as Headteacher at the tiny school at Southernknowe, midway up the College Valley. With it went the schoolhouse at Coldburn, half a mile further up past the school, and we moved there about 12th January 1929.

This is where my childhood began as I remember nothing of Belford. Indeed my earliest memory is of our arrival at Southernknowe and of being carried up to Coldburn by Mr.Cavers through the snow, and wrapped in his shepherd tartan plaid.

Coldburn was to be my home until September 1938, when I passed the 'Scholarship' and went off to the Duchess' School in Alnwick, returning to Coldburn each weekend. The final break from the valley came in 1941, when Dad was directed into war work at Allan Bros., Tweedmouth - the Woodyard.

But College Valley will always be a special place for me - and for my family - my North Country.

HOME.........

Home was to be Coldburn. I suppose the best place to begin is with my memories of our arrival. I do not know how we moved - all I remember is deep snow and arriving at Southernknowe. The farm there was owned by the Cavers family - Mr.Jimmy Cavers, Mrs.Cavers, their son, Anthony(Anty) and his wife Jessie.

Jessie always lit the school fire so they would have a key and doubtless they had the key for our 'new' house at Coldburn.

Because of the cold weather and the fact that Coldburn must have been unoccupied for some time, they insisted we stay the night with them until we could get up next morning and get the fires lit. We had their 'best' bedroom and were made very welcome. Next morning up I went in the tartan plaid. How the furniture got there I do not know unless the van and driver stayed there too.

But more about the Cavers family in a later chapter.

The very name – Coldburn – and the idea of arriving in the snow brings a shiver to the spine. It sounds really inhospitable. It was not so. The hill adjacent, where I spent many happy times, gave it its name. It was a stone cottage in a hollow with a walled garden and sheltered from the winds by a belt of trees. It must have been at least Victorian as it existed before Southernknowe School opened in 1854, but I know nothing of its history.

Downstairs were two rooms – a living room with an old-fashioned black range and a sitting room with a coal fire. There was a kitchen with a sink and running cold water. There was as well a scullery cum vestibule containing a paraffin stove for cooking, while the living room range doubled up as a cooker. Some of these ranges had a tank with a tap giving running hot water, ours did not and we had a kettle on the range permanently.

Upstairs were two bedrooms reached by a ladder. I might add that it was quickly replaced by a staircase which Dad fitted. Mum could not be regarded as slim, and a ladder was not suitable for her. Lighting was by paraffin lamps and candles. I kept two of the old lamps and had one refurbished and converted to electricity after we moved to Stockport and it lights our dining room. We had no bathroom at first so we had to use a tin bath in front of the fire, filled by kettles of hot water. In time, Dad took a piece off the sitting room to make a bathroom with toilet and washbasin, and he also replaced the black range with a Triplex range. With that done, we were much better off for facilities than many in the 1930s.

Like all the valley houses, we had a garden, walled against predatory sheep. Dad grew things capable of withstanding the harsh climate and which would help with winter feeding. Coldburn had been occupied before us and the garden was in quite good order. As well as vegetables, there were fruit bushes – blackcurrants, raspberries and gooseberries, and rhubarb. Winters can be quite severe in the valley. Cheviot often holds a little snow until June. And talking of snow, we were snowed in more than once. Snowed in means blown snow up to the eaves and the dormer windows of the bedrooms. I thought that was lovely, and still do. My husband doesnt see it in the same light – he has to drive the car!.

.....NOT ONLY SHEEP.

I am no historian and my interest is in the people I knew. But settlements in the valley are old, and records of settlements go back for centuries. My husband was interested in the history of the area so he has added a section at the end of the book to deal with the 'boring bits'. But there is one bit of history worth mentioning here. In the Northumberland Record Office, there is a Tithe Map for 1844 when Tithes were abolished and replaced by rents (see the last Chapter) Prior to this, the tenants of Hethpool Estate had to pay 1½d per cow; 4d per 20 ewes; 4d per foal; and 4d per beehive in respect of honey and beeswax. Heather grew profusely in the valley, making honey a valuable taxable item. Incidentally, at Burton, where no heather grew, there were no tithes on beehives, but they paid a 'smoke penny' on every house. Taxes on necessities are not new!

Not only were there a lot of sheep in the valley, but it had other residents, too, even if not many. Starting at the foot of the valley was WESTNEWTON where there were cottages and the 'big house' owned by the Lambton family. I never classed Westnewton as part of the valley which for me began at HETHPOOL, where there were cottages with lovely gardens, and the 'big house' which the Sutherland family occupied. The present house dates from 1919 but the site has had a house for centuries and a pele tower – a house fortified as a defence against the centuries of Border lawlessness.

In the valley proper the first house was WHITEHALL, owned then by Ralph Mack and his wife who had no family that I recall. A little further up was the wooden bungalow used by Miss Pease as a holiday home. She had a great interest in the children and the school and was a benefactor to them. I had a great regard for her and more about her later.

At the point where the valley road splits to diverge up the College and Lambden Burns was the Cuddystone. It was a stone to enable the less active to climb on to their horses. Why it was there I have no idea. At that point is now the Village Hall which was built after I left the valley. Taking the left fork and following the Lambden Burn, you reach SOUTHERNKNOWE and then COLDBURN.

A mile further, past the screes known as the Glidders and over the burn you reach DUNSDALE. The tenant there was Walter Bertram and his wife, Mary. They had sons, Jimmy, John, Robert and George, and Walter's father lived with them. He was Jimmy Bertram (Jimmy Onnyway). He had a curious habit of qualifying everything he said with 'onnyway'. I went to school with the Bertram lads until the family left the valley and moved to Sandy-house, Milfield. The Bertrams were succeeded by the Daggs.

Jack Dagg, like Walter Bertram, was the shepherd there. They lived there throughout the War and their involvement in the rescue of American airmen who had crashed on Cheviot is documented elsewhere. A memorial has been put there. Jack Dagg was an accomplished musician, playing the fiddle, accordian and Northumbrian small pipes. His son, John, kept on the musical tradition and had a Band. He lives in Milfield. Jack and Maggie Dagg had three daughters, Jean, Margaret and Belle. They came to College from the Coquet, and left long after us, moving to Hounam. Margaret returned to live in Wooler and is well known in the area both for her work for the community and as a long time Bus Driver with the 'United' there. Still on Dunsdale, I believe the family there before Bertrams, and therefore before my time, were called Wilson. I recall being told that they emigrated and having more bits and pieces than they could take – china, etc. they buried it somewhere near the house!

Above Dunsdale, the last house is GOLDSCLEUGH. Andrew Newlands was the shepherd there, and they had sons Andrew and John and daughter, Jean. They were older than me, young adults. One son became a shepherd and the other a Policeman. I think they, too, moved across the Border. On a visit to Yetholm in December 1994, I was lucky enough to find and meet Jean Newlands (Mrs.Blacklock) I had not seen her since the mid 1930s. She told me she had walked over the hill from Goldscleugh to Wooler regularly, carrying butter and eggs for sale. The Newlands family were long time residents in the valley. An Andrew Newlands and his family lived at Goldscleugh when the 1881 Census was taken. That Andrew was born in 'Scotland' and had come to the valley as a young shepherd. He was living at Mounthooly at the 1861 Census. They had also lived at Elsdonburn. So the Newlands were probably the valley's longest residents. There were other families at Goldscleugh but I cannot recall in what order. There were Laings whose family I cannot bring to mind or even if they had a family. The others were the Cowens, Dan and Mary, who eventually retired to the 'Pop Inn', otherwise Humbleton.

Returning to the present day Village Hall, the other road follows the College Burn going first to FLEEHOPE, then occupied by Jack Oliver and his wife. They moved away and the Goodfellows took over. They had two sons, Jimmy and John, who attended Southernknowe School after I left. That family subsequently moved to Southernknowe Farm and Mrs.Goodfellow helped Mum, who by then was not in good health, with her housework.
The last house up the College Burn was MOUNTHOOLY, where the Little family lived. Four of that family, Wattie, Mabel, Ellen and Mattie, went to school with me. They were still at Mounthooly when we left, and some of them still live in the Wooler area.
On another farm track from Hethpool was TROWBURN. I do not recall who lived there earlier, but by the time I went to the Duchess' School, the family there were the Browns. They had sons Peter and Ian who attended Southernknowe School. Mrs.Brown later moved to Whittingham and Peter joined the Police at Birmingham.
There were other farms over towards Yetholm, one was ELSDON BURN and the other ELSDONBURNSHANK. The Buchanan family lived at the latter and they visited us from time to time to use the Library, etc. They had a son, Danny, and a daughter, Agnes.

NOT ONLY THE SHEEP AND THE RESIDENTS BUT ALSO....

The 'hired lads'. They came to farms where the shepherd had no sons of the right age to help him. I cannot remember them all but two remain clearly in my mind – Billy Patterson and Ernie Bertram. When we moved to Coldburn, Billy Patterson was hired lad with the Bertram family at Dunsdale. He was another local musician.
Billy 'Pat' moved over Coldburn Hill to be shepherd at Commonburn and married Peg Woodcock from Pallinsburn. He was replaced by Ernie Bertram, nephew to the shepherd, Walter Bertram.

Ernie stayed at Dunsdale until Walter's son, Jimmy, was old enough to shepherd, when he left the valley and moved to Ford. He married Hannah and after their retirement they took over as Caretaker/Guides at the Lady Waterford Hall there. Hannah Bertram died in 1984 and Ernie in 1988, both are buried at Ford. They had two sons, one went into forestry and the other, Alan, joined the Metropolitan Police, from which he retired not so long ago.

My own family produced its contribution to the Police, too. My eldest sister, Winnie, had trained in Dairy work at Newton Rigg College, Penrith. In 1947, she joined the Northumberland Police as one of its first policewomen. She was PW3, and her friend, Audrey Yule, from Berwick was PW2. After her retirement from the Police, she took over as Matron of the Police Training Centre at Dishforth, Yorkshire. She moved to Baldersby and died in 1978.

Talking of Billy Patterson reminds me of an interesting incident. Billy was on Coldburn Hill with his dog in deep snow on the way to our house on a dark winters night. At one point his dog became very excited and seemed to want to stop him. Eventually it came round in front of him and put its paws up on him to stop him going further. He prodded the ground directly in front of him with his stick which promptly sank into deep snow. Somehow the dog knew there was a crevasse there, and it saved his life. He would never part with that collie.

Apart from the sheep, the residents and the hired lads, there were the landowners. I mentioned that the valley was in the hands of the Sutherland family who were there between 1918 and 1936. They had Hethpool House more or less as a holiday home. I never saw them and never remember them coming up the valley, obviously they would do so. The Lambton family from Westnewton were frequent visitors, well known to everybody. Most often it was Capt. Claude Lambton and his daughter, Barbara, who came. Sometimes they had tea with us and Winnie was invited to Westnewton House.

There had been other houses in the valley in the past and for which I had to look into history. There was a Northumberland Map published by Armstrong and Son in 1769. It shows all the houses I have mentioned, except Coldburn, plus others gone by my time. They include Shorthope, Fawcett, Harrowlaws and Boag.

But there is one missing – Firgarth – which does not appear on any map. It was somewhere in the woods across the College Burn from

Whitehall – or perhaps a bit further north. Only some stones marked the place where it had stood. It was supposed to have been occupied by a hermit, of whom I know nothing.

College has other legends. 'Black Adam', the reiver – a sheep rustler – is said to have lived in a cave in Hen Hole, a ravine on the side of Cheviot. Another says that the Hermit of Warkworth lived at Hethpool, but my favourite – and the legend is a bit hazy – concerns a young woman who had eloped only to be followed by her brother. When he caught up with the couple, he is said to have killed his sister accidentally in the ensuing fight. This may be the legend which says there is an area of bracken near Hethpool growing in the shape of a heart representing the grave of Isabella of Widdrington, killed there.

Being so near the Border and on some of the old drove roads, College seems to be just the place for legends. But we must return to more earthly things!.

THE DAILY GRIND

I learnt this song as a child in the valley. I do not know who wrote the words but it is sung to a tune called 'Nellie Gray', the same as that for 'Keep yor feet still. Geordie hinny'.

'Oh!, there's songs about our soldiers and our sailors by the score,
 Of tinkers and of tailors and of other men galore,
 But I sing you now a ditty you have never heard before,
 Of the canny shepherd laddies of the hills.'
Chorus:–
'O! the shepherds of the Coquet, of the Alwin and the Rede,
 The Bowmont and the Breamish, they are all of the same breed,
 With their collie dogs behind them and a stick with a horn heid,
 The canny shepherd laddies of the hills.

We know all about the shepherds, but what about their families? What did they contribute and what were their lives like?

The shepherds' wives had a hard and busy life and children had to learn the work ethic at an early age. Everybody had to contribute.

In the 1930s, life in the towns was often very hard, with housing conditions far from superb. Families lived in one or two rooms in crowded yards. My husband was brought up in Berwick in a 'yard'.

Working women!. Mum with a sickle; Me with a rake: and Winnie with the 'clooty' mat. At Coldburn c.1939.

Working women!
Milking.

At the pole formerly at the summit of Cheviot. Collies and shepherds. Ernie and Jimmy Bertram at the front.

The frontage to that property had, and I think still has the lead drainpipe bearing the date 1779. He can remember Sallyport with a tenement housing about 60 people and reputed to have only one toilet. Life in the remoteness of Cheviot was less convenient in lacking proximity to shops, cinemas, etc., but better in other respects as it was good clean air and the housing conditions were far superior to many of those I have just mentioned in Berwick. We had a bathroom – my husband used a tin bath in the kitchen.

The houses in the Valley were at least as big as Coldburn, perhaps bigger. In my time they all had running water, and gardens, and they seemed to have been well maintained. So life was generally healthy. Childhood ailments rife in the towns pre–war were non–existent. To a degree that was detrimental. My husband had measles, chickenpox and whooping cough – I did not, nor did the other children – but I caught measles when I went to school in Alnwick aged 11. The standard of health is well illustrated by Jimmy Bertram from Dunsdale, who would be about 4 years older than me. When he left Southernknowe School aged 14, he had never had a days absence, despite the 3 mile daily walk, and the need to help for example with the farm work. In bad weather he carried his younger brother to and from school on his back. Such was his record that the Northumberland Education Committee gave him a Certificate and a gold watch.

So, what about the day?. The womens' work revolved around housekeeping and looking after the animals. These are hill sheep farms and life had to circulate around the needs of the animals, taking complete priority. As well as the sheep, each house except ours kept two cows, one or two pigs, hens, and a horse and cart, and the all important collies.

Rising time was about 0500/0600 depending on the season – and that was well before daybreak in winter. First a quick cup of tea before cleaning, laying and lighting the fires, including, on washing day, the copper boiler. The men went straight out to see to the animals. Lambing time was the busiest time of all when sleep was at a premium and thus tempers easily frayed. The men went out on foot so they had to cover a wide area when the animals had not been brought 'in–bye' as in inclement weather. Once the fires were lit, the women had to bring in and feed any sickly animals. At lambing, weakly lambs might be there already, even needing overnight attention. There were always the hens and pigs to be fed as well as the cattle in winter.

By about 0730, the men would be back and everybody had a big breakfast of porridge and bacon and egg. The men went out again and would be on the hills until midday. They might call in mid-morning for a mug of tea, or they might take a 'piece' with them. Once they had gone the children had to be got ready for school. That meant self-help as there was not time enough to do things which the children could do themselves, or that the older children could do for the others. There was also a role for the elderly relatives here. Grannies were an asset in doing all kinds of jobs.

Most of the daily work dealing with animals other than sheep was for the wives. Just what that entailed and the order in which it was done was governed by the seasons. The cows had to be milked before breakfast. In summer they stayed out overnight and had to be brought in for milking, but being the intelligent animals they are, they knew exactly when to come 'in-bye'. In winter, when they were inside, their stalls had to be cleaned out first and everything disinfected. For milking they used the traditional three-legged stool which hung in the byre. The cows always had fresh hay or cattle cake while they were being milked. They, too, have their own personalities and can be co-operative or awkward at milking!. The order was to bring a bucket of warm, soapy water and wash the udder and clean the cow generally. For the milk they used another bucket, previously scalded out to be sterile. The milk was taken to the dairy at the house. It was poured through a clean muslin cloth into another sterilised bucket in order to remove any foreign matter like cows hair. One needed a lot of hot water, not only for the sterilisation, but also for washing the muslin, all of this water had to be boiled in the house – so fires were needed all year. The farm cats always came to the milking to get a saucer of milk The cats were not domestic pets, but working animals necessary to keep vermin at bay. Once milked, the cows were turned out again in summer. Then the wife had to clean out the stall again or she might leave that job until later. The milk was taken to the farmhouse, each of which had a scullery with running water where work was done and a separate dairy were food was stored. Once into the dairy, the milk was cooled in something resembling an old fashioned rubbing board but with pipes through which cold water was run to cool the milk quickly. After cooling, some was put aside for daily use and some into flattish earthenware bowls – crocks – brown on the outside and cream coloured on the inside. They were then left on a cold stone shelf to stand until evening by which time the cream had risen to the top. Using a big flat spoon with holes in it, the cream was then skimmed off. It was transferred to another container and put aside to make butter. The residual (skimmed) milk was used for scones, soda bread, etc. and the surplus fed to the pigs and ferrets. These processes were repeated after the evening milking and the skimming was done 12 hours later in each case.

Digressing, I mentioned feeding ferrets. I know the Cavers family kept two to keep the rabbit population in check, but I do not know about the other families. They were nasty, vicious little creatures and I never went near them nor indeed would the Cavers' ever let me near them.

In describing the milking, I have got away from the order of the day. Bear in mind that milking and the related jobs were done twice daily by the women. After the morning milking the housework had to be done. Beds had to be made and the house cleaned daily. There were no vacuum cleaners and everything had to be done by hand. 'Clooty' mats had to be lifted, taken out, and shaken. They were not light. Floors were of wood or flagstones and had to be swept daily. Only in the best room was there linoleum. The men and children came home in dirty boots, not into the house, but into the entrance, where outdoor footwear stayed. That had to be washed often, and the dairy had to be kept spotlessly clean. Oil lamps were the norm – they had to be filled, have the wicks trimmed, and the glass globes cleaned regularly. Having always been used to oil lamps, I did not find them unpleasant, but if they were not kept in good order and allowed to smoke, they made nasty black marks on the ceiling.

Older children did these jobs, me included.

Days were set aside for certain jobs. Monday was always washing day. The copper boiler in the washhouse had to be lit early to heat the large quantity of hot water for washing and rinsing, as well as boiling garments. Washing was a full days work and Mondays dinner had to be cold meat from the Sunday joint. There were no electric machines to bung everything in and leave it to look after itself. Washing was done in a big wooden tub filled with hot soapy water. The garments were first 'possed' with a wooden poss stick to knock the dirt out of them. They were then taken out one by one and scrubbed on a scrubbing board. Now the water is hot and it is hard on the hands. White articles were then transferred to the copper boiler and boiled, while others went back into the poss tub for further 'treatment'. Between each process they had to be mangled by hand. The mangle was on a stand above the poss tub so that the soapy water mangled out went back into the tub for the next lot of washing. Remember that the copper had to be filled by hand, lit and brought to the boil. Each lot of washing had to be graded so that the least dirty were done first to minimise the use of hot water. There were no detergents as we know them, although 'Rinso' came on to the market. We used soft soap and soda and on the scrubbing board, big blocks of hard green 'Fairy' soap.

For the more delicate articles, Mum used 'Lux' pure soap flakes. Soap takes a lot of rinsing out. I used to help Jessie Cavers with the washing at Southernknowe Farm sometimes. She used to sing a rhyme about soft soap and soda. 'Some people say I have a lisp, but I can not perceive it : I can say green soap, white soap, soft soap and soda'. Wet Mondays were hated. Washing was festooned everywhere and there seemed to be a perpetual cloud of steam.

Tuesday was ironing day, using either flat irons heated on the fire or we had a box iron with a built-in container into which was dropped a metal bolt pre-heated on the fire. Heat could not be regulated – other than by experience, and it was very easy to scorch things. Conversely it could make the ironing of starched things difficult. No, there was no tinned spray starch nor easy-care polycottons – it was just plain hard labour. Linen tablecloths were kept for Sundays and woe betide anybody who spilt anything on them! Otherwise, table covers for general use were of oilcloth, easily wiped down.

The main meal was midday dinner, which, apart from Monday's cold meat, was a good meal with, maybe, soup then some kind of meat – pork if a pig had been killed, or mince or a stew, etc. with vegetables – fresh, not frozen, which had not been invented – then a pudding. This might be a rice or a steamed pudding. Dinner was eaten about 12 noon, and meat was a vital part. No one was vegetarian then. We were the exception, not having midday dinner. As Mum was teaching and Dad away at work, we had to have dinner after school on schooldays.

Baking was done on two or three days each week, sometimes more.

Many made bread as well as the soda bread which was easier and quicker to make, and, of course, scones. They were always excellent, and skimmed or sour milk was often used. Even today, I never throw away sour milk but use it to make the best scones. Then they made various cakes and fruit or jam tarts. It was usual to have a good baking session and fill up the cake tins. Again there was an element of discipline in the order of baking because you would be using a coal fired oven which had to be regulated by experience. Mum always had a good baking afternoon in my time and I have continued the practice although I am luckier in having deep freezers to house the products. My daughter does the same and is never without quality cakes.

Another important job for the women was butter making. It took place once or twice a week depending on the weather and the supply of cream. Margarine was available but it was viewed as an inferior product and when you had a supply of milk you kept to butter. The butter churn stood in the dairy. First of all it had to be scalded out, cooled, and clean muslin put over the bung, even though it would have been put away clean. The churn, which has removable paddles inside, has to be turned by hand in a regular rythm and not with a jerky movement. As the churn turns, the cream turns to butter and after about half an hour you can hear the sound change from a sloshing noise to more of a bump, telling you there is something solid among the liquid in the churn. That comes only with experience, and when it is ready, the bung is withdrawn carefully, and the residual buttermilk drained off into a clean dish or enamel bucket. Jessie Cavers used to put clean cold water into the churn to wash out the buttermilk and clean the churn. The butter was then put on a flat wooden slab to be pressed and patted to remove the remaining liquid. Salt was then added by turning over in layers and salting each layer. With wooden butter pats, dipped frequently in cold water, the butter was shaped into blocks with a pattern imprinted in the top using the edges and corners of the butter pats. All the equipment was then scrubbed and scalded before being put away ready for the next time. Nowadays you can see this process at working farm museums like that at Acton Scott near Shrewsbury, our favourite and one where many of the old style processes are done. Just imagine the time it takes to do this. Half an hour to turn the churn, how long to salt and pat and then to clean? I used to help Jessie Cavers to make butter. It was another time she taught me a rhyme to keep the churn turning at a constant rate. It went...'I'm h-a-p-p-y, I'm h-a-p-p-y, I think I am, I know I am, I'm h-a-p-p-y'. This was one of many.

The women still had to fit the preparation of meals around these jobs. The men came in mid afternoon, about 3.30pm for tea and a scone or cake, so baking had to be ready for that. Supper was eaten about 7-8pm. That might be cold boiled bacon, pickles, etc., and on some days it would be a social occasion, of which more later. But between tea and supper there were other tasks. The cows and hens had to be fed and eggs gathered. Sticks, coal, and peat had to be brought in for next morning and time had to be found to do the garden.

After supper, there was sewing and mending to be done, and the thick woollen socks to be darned. In winter 'clooty' mats were made and there were then limited leisure activities which I will relate in another section.

Another job for the women was decorating the house. Usually the rooms were distempered. At Coldburn, we used distemper on to which was added a decorative paper border, something which has come back into fashion in recent times. Our present home in Stockport was built in 1914. We redecorated the staircase not so long ago, and having peeled off the old wallpaper, it revealed yellow distemper with a decorative stepped border of many years ago. Also at Coldburn we did have eventually wallpaper on the sitting room and living room walls. I do not know if it was done elsewhere - I suppose it was.

About sanitation - in my time all the houses in the valley were refurbished and had bathrooms added. That was done when I was a small child and I cannot remember the other houses as they had been. At Coldburn, Dad took a piece off the sitting room to make a bathroom with toilet and handbasin. That was connected to a septic tank. Before that, like everybody else, we had an outside toilet - a 'nettie'. It had a wooden front behind which was a bucket, and the toilet top extended from wall to wall across the outhouse. The bucket had to be emptied frequently, a job for the men or the older boys to dispose of the contents on to the dung heap and eventually back to the fields or gardens. It had to be scrubbed out weekly. Mum had to scrub out the school 'nettie' every week, too Of course, we had to have potties for night use – it wasnt ideal to have to go out in the small hours when snow was on the ground!.

STILL MORE OF THE DAILY GRIND......

Returning to 'The Canny Shepherd Laddies of the Hills', the last verse goes:–

'I've said no word about their wives, but I think their is no need,
Because in every house I've been, they always are the heid,
But I think you'll all agree with me, it takes good wives to breed
The canny shepherd laddies of the hills.'

So, some recognition by the writer!.

Not part of everyday life, but something which took place regularly, was the pig killing. All the farms kept pigs and from time to time, each farm killed one. Not being shepherds or farmers, we did not keep pigs, and I never attended a pig killing so I am not that well qualified to relate what happened.
It was not a pleasant task and I would not have wanted to go. It was usually done in the morning and the children would be at school. As well as the shepherd, two or three other shepherds would come to assist and one of them would know how to butcher the meat. A relative, Mrs.Nellie Cock, who always lived in north Northumberland, but not the College Valley,told me something about it recently, of which I'll spare you the gory details.
As I have said, the killing was done in the morning, and the carcase was hung from a ladder for some time and then cleaned. The next day the carcase was cut up and the joints salted, using a stick to push salt into the joints to ensure the meat was properly cured and thus would not 'go off'. The offal was removed and cleaned and at this stage black pudding, oatmeal pudding, and sausage would be made. The pig's head was boiled and used to make potted meat. There were no fridges and those items had to be made as soon as possible. Another of the wives would come in that day to help.
Once the carcase was cool and salted, a board was laid down, covered with straw and then with a clean white sheet. The joints of meat were laid on this sheet and again rubbed with salt. They were

then covered by this sheet and left to cure for about 10 days. The cover was then opened and the joints turned. More salt might be applied and the cover replaced for another 10 days. The cured pork was then wrapped in muslin to keep the flies off it, hung up from hooks in the kitchen ceiling, and brown paper placed on the floor to catch any drips. As a child, Nellie was warned not to walk underneath the meat as if any salt dripped on to her head, her hair would fall out!. I can bear this out as I was also told that when I went to another valley house after a pig killing.

The house would have more sausage and offal than they could use. Each neighbour would be given sausage, spare ribs, liver, etc., to use them up, and this was reciprocated when the other houses did their pig killing. We were always given some at Coldburn. I must say I did not like the fat, salted bacon!

Sheep shearing time was another busy spell for the women. The shepherds helped each other and the women had to cater for the extra hands at their place for the shearing, so much extra cooking. When I was young, I went over to Southernknowe Farm straight after school daily – while Mum was clearing up – and helped Mrs.Cavers and Jessie with some or other of their jobs. I was always given a glass of milk and something to eat. It might be blackcurrant tart (my favourite) or freshly baked scones or rice pudding kept back from dinnertime. It is still a lovely memory.

But Mrs.Cavers or Jessie baked every day – not only for the family but also as they had a hired lad to feed. When all the household and farm jobs had been done, there was always knitting or sewing or mending waiting. The living rooms had oilcloth on the floors. There were no fitted carpets and everybody made their own mats – 'clooty mats'. They were either 'hooky' or 'proggy', and this was the job for the winter nights when outside work was reduced.

The 'hooky' mats were made with short strips of material hooked through the base material and each knotted. The' proggy' ones were made from long strips prodded through and back again through the base. They were usually patterned so the material had to be sorted in advance, and this was the job for the children. The material was whatever was discarded from other uses – the good parts of worn out clothing, for example, as nothing was wasted. It had to be heavier material and not cotton which would not last in the heavy wear these mats took.

For the base of the mat sacking from the animal feedstuff bags was used. It had to be washed, dried, and cut to size.

Flour and oatmeal were bought in sacks for the winter. The small sacks for these items were made from unbleached calico. It was washed and put out to dry on gorse bushes – so it did not blow away, and there it was bleached by the sun. It was then cut up, hemmed, and used, sometimes for tea towels, but also embroidered for use as teacloths. Mum had a Singer treadle sewing machine. Most of the houses had a sewing machine – some were small and hand operated. 'Clooty' mats have made a revival and they are quite expensive in the craft shops. But they are 'labour intensive'. They are one of the real folk crafts, often exhibited at the annual Shows; another is the Northumbrian quilt but I did not see them made by anyone in the valley.

Moving on to bedding, chaff beds were commonly used and I had one. They were made from striped featherproof ticking, bought in. They are just bags filled with chaff from the corn. I was asked 'are they prickly?'. Well, I dont remember if they were.

There were no arable farms in the valley and threshing was done at Kirknewton or nearby. The annual threshing was the time for a new chaff bed and the chaff mattresses were emptied out. The men took the empty cases down on their cart and refilled these cases with new chaff. So the contents were replaced annually. When the bed was newly refilled, it was quite fluffy and you seemed to be lying in bed almost up to the ceiling. In time it settled down and was much more compacted when it was due for replacement.

The chaff bed lay on a straw mattress. These mattresses were made from hessian filled with compressed straw and were fastened to the bed itself. They were bought, not home made.

My chaff bed was later replaced by a feather bed. Mine may have been bought in, but everybody kept feathers. When a hen was killed for food and plucked, the feathers were wrapped in brown paper and put into the oven on the coal range and left there for some time until they were sterilised. They were then used to fill cushions.

They were better at recycling then we are now.

PUFF BALLS AND CAMPHORATED OIL.

Talking about chaff beds brings me to think that they could not have been good for anyone with back trouble, but what about health in general? I should have liked to write something about health and how we coped with illness, but in fact I have little recollection of much illness.

The local doctor was Dr.Jaboor from Wooler. He came up when necessary but those were the days before the National Health Service, and doctors had to be paid. They were not called unless it was vitally necessary. To summon him, somebody had to go down to Westnewton by bike to phone him as there was no phone in the valley. Despite drinking lots of full cream milk – straight from the cow – and eating butter and fat bacon, things now considered grossly unhealthy, there was not the incidence of heart disease. The only casualty I can remember was Anthony Cavers, who died from a heart attack, aged 49. He was slim, athletic and had been a fell runner. In his latter days with deteriorating health, he did his shepherding on horseback.

We had our own health problems when Mum developed a heart complaint also when I was at Alnwick, and a doctor was called then, followed by a nurse. Mum had paid into a medical insurance to cover this possibility and in any case we moved to Berwick shortly afterwards where we had easier access to medical services.

We all had cuts and bruises and other relatively minor complaints and we just got on with them. I had, myself, only one unpleasant incident when a pan of hot water was pulled over, scalding my arm badly. Jack Oliver came over from Fleehope and applied to the scald a mixture of pure lard and puffball and the scald healed. He must have had to go out and find a puffball, and I wonder how he would have treated it outside the mushroom time.

For a sore throat, you were given small balls of butter rolled in sugar and for chesty colds and coughs, camphorated oil was rubbed in then covered with a piece of flannel. Brown paper was used in place of flannel too. Mum used honey and lemon and a lovely cough medicine – 'Liquoricine'. She administered syrup of figs once, with disastrous results – never again! That was a usual remedy in those days, so were senna pods.

Mum believed in prevention, and I had 'Virol' malt extract daily in winter. It was nice. I dont know what other remedies were used by the farming families, but I have heard of odd things like wrapping bacon fat round the neck!

PIGS POTATOES AND OTHER DELICACIES.

Shopping forays were not so common – you made or grew or killed what you needed and vans came up, as did travelling drapers. If you wanted to go shopping you went to Wooler or Yetholm or maybe Berwick. The subject of transport will be dealt with later; suffice it to say that it was something you provided yourself and you had not much time to visit shops.

A lot of meat, eggs, butter, bread and scones were on the menu. The purchases that were vital were flour, sugar, oatmeal and the like – things which could be stored for use in the bad weather, and these were stocked up each autumn.

We got our autumn supplies from Scott the mealmaker in High Street, Berwick, a dark shop full of sacks, the tops of which were rolled back to reveal everything from oatmeal to dog biscuits. It had a distinctive, but not unpleasant smell. As Dad had a motor bike and sidecar, he and Mum went to Yetholm for the regular shopping. She said there was a good grocer there – that was Mr. Armstrong, where she said you could get everything you needed. His shop in the main street of Town Yetholm has gone, and the building is now a guest house, the Paramount Guest House.

Mum kept a supply of tinned milk, both evaporated and condensed, for all year use; winter for bad weather, otherwise for baking. She made coconut haystacks with condensed milk; they were tasty.

We kept only hens, but the other houses kept two cows; one in milk and one in calf, and a heifer calf. If there was a temporary shortage of milk at one house, there was always a supply available from another. We got our milk from either Dunsdale or Southernknowe. All the farms kept pigs and two were killed each year at each place. I have related something about the pig killing already and merely repeat that some of the proceeds of that were circulated through the valley. Eggs and hens were a useful food source. Hens dont oblige by laying on a regular daily basis; there are times of surplus and shortage, the latter in winter. Thus when there was a surfeit, they were preserved. Everybody says they were preserved in isinglass. I made enquiries about it and what was used was in fact waterglass, a chemical, sodium silicate. It came from the grocers in red and blue tins. I did not find preserved eggs nice to eat and Mum used them only for baking. The fresh eggs were placed in an earthenware crock or a bucket, in layers, carefully. The waterglass, a powder, was dissolved in boiling water, allowed to cool and poured over the eggs, making an airtight seal around each eggshell. The preservative had a consistency of wallpaper paste and each egg had to be well washed before use. It was always prudent to break them individually as one or two might have gone off.

As well as garden vegetables, Mum used nettles, either boiled as a vegetable or made into nettle tea. They are full of iron.

Two vans came up from the Glendale Co-op in Wooler. Jimmy Redpath drove the flat truck with a tarpaulin cover which came up every fortnight bringing groceries and meat. Jack Fairnington drove the bakery van. He came every Wednesday, as well as bakery items he had a few sweets. Jack was one of the oldest of a large family and some days he brought one or two of his younger brothers with him. One told me recently that on one journey with Jack, he and his brother had to travel in the back of the van. There were cakes there, and they ate some of the icing off the cakes. Jack was furious when he found the cakes. 'How the hell do you expect me to sell those cakes if there's no icing on them?'

The Fairnington boys stayed at Coldburn sometimes, but one of them suffered from a calcium deficiency causing brittle bones. He was always falling and fracturing them. He would not drink milk so Mum spread condensed milk on bread and called it milk jam. He ate that and it may have helped. I think his condition improved.

Apart from the limited range of sweets brought by the Co-op van, we had little access to shops for sweets. Neither did we have ice cream in the valley. There were no freezers and no ice cream vans.

All the houses had a garden and the priority was to grow crops which could be stored, especially for winter use. Dad grew potatoes, early and maincrop, the traditional varieties like Arran Pilot and Kerr's Pink; carrots, swedes; onions; leeks; and for summer use, cabbage and cauliflower. He always planted potatoes at Easter for harvesting earlies at Race Week. Now since Easter is a movable feast and Race Week fixed, I find it odd how he managed to get them ready.

Potato peelings were boiled and fed to the pigs and other scraps went as pig swill. Another delicacy prepared for the pigs were the so-called 'pigs potatoes'. They were the small potatoes, too small to be kept for storage. They were boiled in a big pan, unwashed,

The baker's van – Jack Fairnington and brothers. c.1931.

Above– Nellie MacLain leading a hay pike.

Below – a touch of winter!

and when cooked, the water drained off them and allowed to cool. That was done before the children came home from school. We all went straight to the pan and helped ourselves, removing the skins from the cooked potatoes and eating them – with butter – if you got the chance. They were not special to the valley and most country children must have had them. Many never reached the pigs!.

All gardens had fruit bushes which the women looked after, from which much jam was made and fruit bottled. This was done on the traditional method with kilner jars, very successful but you got scalded fingers in the process. We also picked the bilberries which grew wild in profusion, using jam jars with string round the top to carry them. They were made into tarts. Picking them was a time consuming job so it went to the children. We like them and each summer we go over to Sutton Bank in Yorkshire where we think the best grow. There are also brambles and wild crab apples, the latter used to make apple or bramble jelly.

We did have fish sometimes. As far as I know it was legal to take trout from the burn and the boys could take them by 'tickling' them. In August, the boys caught the trout they called 'whitlings'. I can not define exactly what they are as I never fished for them myself. I did love the trout, fresh from the burn, when Mum cleaned them, rolled them in oatmeal and fried them. They were delicious and totally different from todays farmed trout. We had salmon, too, and they were not caught legally!. The men went out for them at night, carrying gaffs (sticks with hooks on the end) to grab the salmon, first having attracted and dazzled them with carbide lamps.

We visited an elderly lady in Wooler recently. Before her marriage she lived at Westnewton in a ground floor house, whose upper floor was reached by an outside stone staircase. In the upper flat lived Ernie Bertram. Jean and her mother had not yet gone to bed when they heard footsteps on the stairs outside. Mother said, 'Ernie is away out late tonight, there'll be a cut of salmon in the morning'. Sure enough there was!.

ALL MOD CONS......

We used paraffin lamps for lighting and some had paraffin stoves as back up to their coal range. It was delivered by Jimmy Redpath on the Co-op van. But we also used a lot of coal. In those days it was the normal fuel and there was seen to be 'good' and 'bad' coal. Coal from Shilbottle was preferred to that from Scremerston, but I have no idea where our supply came from. It was not delivered to the door, but by train to Kirknewton Station on some agreed date, not often, so you had to plan how much you would need. The valley men went down by horse and cart and led it back up. We did not have to go down ourselves and we had no suitable transport for it, so somebody brought it up for us, thankfully. But coal needed sticks and they had to be chopped by the men and the biggest boys and brought in daily. Firewood was collected and dried, but Dad, being a joiner, always had dry bits about.

We also burnt peat, and everybody, including the children had to help with digging and carrying. Nowadays you will see it being dug and dried in Scotland and it is not thought of as being a Northumbrian fuel. It has to be dug in 'slices' using a special long narrow spade then laid aside to dry when it was loaded on to horse-drawn sledges and taken to the farm steading to be built into a stack and kept as dry as possible. It is hard work which must be done early in summer to allow the maximum drying time. Mind you, a peat fire burns slowly, giving off excellent heat and a nice aroma.

So much for the main fuels, coal, peat and paraffin. There was no electricity in the valley in our time, nor was there town gas. Central heating was available by placing a paraffin stove in the middle of the floor. These were the days before nationalisation.

Telephones were also absent from the valley. The nearest public telephone was at Westnewton, so even in an emergency, somebody had to ride down there to get help. Given an emergency in bad weather ; serious illness, etc., then hard luck. You had to wait.

A phone box was installed at Southernknowe eventually, but well after our time.

I have said that washing was done by hand, as was cleaning. There were washers and vacuum cleaners available in the 1930s but they were expensive and far beyond the reach of most. Fridges were also uncommon and there were no freezers, so planning of food purchases and storage was vital.

Another of our current necessities, dustbins, were unknown. A lot was recycled, or fed to pigs. Things such as tin cans were first burnt on the fire to sterilise and partly destroy them, then they were buried as was broken china. Great care had to be taken not to

Mr.Cavers unloading the peat sled. It can be pulled by a horse or two men, depending on the terrain. The peat is built into a stack and covered with straw to keep it dry.

Jack Tarbit, the Kirknewton postman, with the mail and his bike. The family, Prue, and a group of visitors at Coldburn. August 1938.

dispose of anything in a manner which could injure the animals – and it was before that horror – the plastic bag – had been invented.

The post was an important part of daily life. The nearest Post Office was at Kirknewton, in the cottage where Jack Tarbit and his wife, Frances, lived. Frances looked after the Post Office while Jack was the postman, riding up the valley daily on a push bike to deliver and collect mail. He also brought up the daily papers. We have a photo of Jack Tarbit and his bike taken at Coldburn. It was hard work for him but the Post Office would be less busy as there were no welfare benefits then and little in the way of pensions. But what you never had, you never missed.

SENSIBLE SHOES AND RECYCLING.

Fashion was not an integral part of the womens' lives. They had Sunday best, but it had to be practical as did footwear.

The women did a lot of knitting and sewing so much was home made. Clothing had to be hard wearing, and all the women wore big wrap–over cotton aprons which were practical garments. Some supplemented these with brown coat overalls to do milking and dairy work, but they didnt wear the 'bratty' aprons used by the field workers. Mrs.Cavers wore a big apron which she could fold over to make a big bag into which she collected eggs. I never knew her break any.

There were no visits to the hairdressers. The women wore their hair in either a bun or a plait. My sister, Winnie, had her hair cut and marcel–waved but that was after she left the valley.

One of the valley men, Jack Oliver, from Fleehope, cut the mens' hair, otherwise they went into Wooler.

Travelling drapers came up, each about twice a year. 'Stocking Willie' came up on a push bike with two big panniers – a right heave up the hill from Westnewton. He brought socks, underwear, aprons etc., in the panniers as well as tweeds which he carried folded up in a big waterproof sheet. The stuff was good quality and hard wearing. The other draper was Mr.John Brown who came from Rothbury and had a car. His stock was similar to Willie's but he carried cotton material too.

All the men wore boots, as did the children – heavy ones for the boys and lighter for the girls. They did their own repairs.

I had boots to be the same as everybody else, but I did have shoes and sandals as well. Mum got my shoes at Alnwick.

Mum was a good seamstress and made a lot of our clothes. I had one cotton dress, white with big red poppies, which she made. I wore it to climb a tree but slipped and tore it from top to bottom on a branch.

Returning to 'Stocking Willie' – he was well known. His name was Willie Robson and he had come from the Swinton area to settle in Yetholm. After retiring, he continued to live in Kirk Yetholm, and died there about 1955/1960. It is only recently that we gave to Beamish Museum a length of heavy tweed that Mum had bought from him to make Dad an overcoat.

Willie brought good quality stuff and could not be faulted for that but he was well known for his 'thrift'. This story was told to me but it would be before our time in the valley. Willie always went about on his bike with the two big panniers but he did go quite far from Yetholm so he used the train from Mindrum Station on the Coldstream – Alnwick branch. This day his calls had been in the Glanton and Whittingham district and he needed the train home. He thought he had time to cycle, not to Glanton Station, but to Hedgeley Station, the next along the line. He missed the train at Hedgeley and cycled on hopefully, first to Wooperton, then to Ilderton, without a chance of catching up with the train. He ended up cycling all the way to Yetholm – but he had saved the 3d!

Thinking back to womens' clothing, one thing they did not wear were trousers, which only came into use during the war. They had to wear thick woollen skirts and thick stockings for protection. Now what about old clothing?. Adult garments made from woollen cloth or cotton which were past wear had the good parts cut out to make clothes for the children. Bits left over after that went into 'clooty' mats. Having been recycled thus, when the childrens' clothes were worn out they went either as dusters or floorcloths or the rags constantly needed to wipe down the cows. Any last vestiges after that were burnt. Bed sheets worn in the middle were split lengthways and sewn up side to side to extend their life; they could also be made into pillowcases. If one side of that wore, it would be turned into a tea towel or dishcloth or to cover food in the larder. A good big piece would be kept to wrap the pig's carcase whilst it was being cured.

34

Knitted woollens past their best were unpicked and unravelled; the good parts were rolled into hanks in the way wool used to be bought. It was then washed and dried carefully to take out the crinkles, then wound into balls and knitted into other garments. There were no such things as J–cloths, dishcloths or yellow dusters. But there was a big demand for cloths for cleaning and everything had to be recycled. Even now, I still keep a box of odds and ends of material. Remember that tables were scrubbed regularly as were pantry shelves and floors in the interests of hygiene. Those horrible sticky flypapers were always used. The preparation of milk, butter and cheese called for hygiene and all were conscious of the need for it.

Recycling of material was time consuming. Many households had elderly relatives unfit to do heavy work, but who were ideal to do this job. They were an asset to a busy family.

PEDAL POWER.

With only a handful of houses in the valley, there was not enough demand to warrant public transport. The valley road was not fit for even small buses, in fact it was not fit for many vehicles, being no more than a track with grass up the middle. The Trow Burn had to be forded. Early in the War, there had been an aircraft crash –one of many – on Cheviot and Dad went down the valley on his motor bike to alert the Police. A group of 6 or 8 Army dispatch riders came on their motor bikes. Dad knew the Trow Burn was treacherous in that it contained a lot of big stones which were moved about by heavy rain. It had to be negotiated with care or you came off your bike. He warned the dispatch riders but they said something about being experts, etc. Dad led them up to the Trow Burn but waited to see them go through. One by one they came through at speed, and one by one they came off into the burn!

There was public transport available at Kirknewton, both bus and train originally. The railway station there was on the Coldstream to Alnwick branch line, and it was 5 miles from Southernknowe. The passenger service was withdrawn early – in 1930 – although goods trains and our coal continued to operate until the line was badly damaged in the floods of 1948. We have a copy of the 1922 Bradshaws Railway Guide. At that time there were three trains on weekdays between Alnwick and Coldstream with connections to and from Berwick. The timetable allowed for a day in Berwick, but that would have been an 'annual event' or even less. With Mum, the schoolchildren and their mothers, I did travel on the last passenger train on this line, having visited Miss Pease at Alnmouth, but more of that later.

As well as the pre−1930 train service, there were buses between Wooler, Kirknewton and Yetholm. They would have been started in the 1920s by an independent busman, Richie Stenhouse of Yetholm. He had other bus services from Yetholm to Kelso and to Berwick. Stenhouse sold his services about 1934; the Kelso route to SMT and the Wooler and Berwick routes to United. We have a United timetable for the summer of 1936 which shows Service 71 running between Wooler and Yetholm on Mondays, Wednesdays, Fridays, Saturdays and Sundays. The Saturday bus service was very good bearing in mind the small population served. It gave a last bus from Wooler to Kirknewton at 11.00pm. The fare for that journey was 6d single and 11d return (2½p and 4½p)

We, ourselves, never used the bus, but it was used by at least some of the valley women who cycled or walked to and from Westnewton to catch it.

Shanks pony was usual. The men often walked to and from Wooler by Commonburn, a 7 mile walk, 4 miles shorter than the road. They also walked to and from Yetholm, going up the Trow Burn and over to Halterburn. As well, they walked over the hills to dances and came back in time to 'look' their sheep next morning.

When we moved into the valley, Dad had a motor bike, and soon added a sidecar which was vital for his work travelling about the county. As far as I know, he was the first to have a motor bike. The hired lads and the young men had push bikes, but some of the older men did not, and must have always walked. The Cavers at Southernknowe had no transport of their own other than a horse and cart. The parents were old; none of the family had bikes and only later, when faced with heart trouble, did Anthony travel on horseback. I am told that the family had been regular attenders at Bowmont Church every Sunday and must have gone by horse and cart. As time went by, the young men got motor bikes and they came to Dad to help with their maintenance.

Transport of the day – Dad's wood could be useful!

THE SOCIAL ROUND.

As I have said, life revolved around the animals and they had priority. The everyday jobs were time-consuming and there was not a lot of time left for leisure. But that did not mean that life was all work and no play. The valley was a community in the fullest sense and without ready access to man-made entertainment, the residents made their own social life.

There were always invitations out to supper at one or other of the houses, but mainly in the darker nights when farm work was less demanding. You got the inevitable cold boiled bacon and pickles, then soda bread, scones and various kinds of cakes. There were always mats to be made and everybody helped with that. You did not go and sit and do nothing. It was also an opportunity to play cards; whist, rummy, and the men played pontoon. The musicians – Jack Dagg, Billy Patterson and others– would come along and play, and the floor might be cleared for Scottish dancing.

When the men went over to Fleehope for Jack Oliver to cut their hair, that was another social occasion for card playing. Then there were dances in the other valleys. I remember Winnie walking over to Uswayford in Coquet to go to a dance.

The hired lads went into Wooler on Saturday nights when work permitted, in early days on foot, later on bikes or motor bikes. I never recall the older men – the householders – doing that. That reminds me of one incident involving one of the hired lads, Ernie Bertram. It was a winter night when there was a knocking on our door at Coldburn. When Mum answered it, there was Ernie, white as a sheet. 'Ay, Mistress Cowe, I've been followed up the road by a ghost. Every time I stopped, it stopped, and every time I walked on, it came.' Mum asked Ernie in and a minute or two later there was a bleating outside our door. It was Prue, our white goat. She had followed Ernie, who had had a little bit to drink! So much for Ernie Bertram's ghost.

Southernknowe School was also the County Library, but Mum kept the library books at Coldburn so they were available at any time and not merely during school hours when everybody was at work. They all read books and non-fiction was more popular than fiction. All were interested in acquiring knowledge and the valley people were all well-read. From time to time people speak to me about a country upbringing and some have said 'oh, they were only shepherds up there!'. I find that attitude infuriating.

Sometimes children would be told to get a book changed for their parents, and Mum did that, knowing individual tastes in reading, but they often came down themselves to change books, making it a social occasion for us.

Mum bought the National Geographical Magazine which she circulated throughout the valley and it was very popular.

Everybody listened to the radio and ours was never off.

We had parties at Christmas. There was always one in the school, for which Miss Pease provided presents, sweets, etc., as well as decorations. We always had a big Christmas tree, but I do not know who supplied that. There was also a Christmas party at Kirknewton School to which we were invited.

There were activities at Easter, too. The Sundays in Lent are known locally as Tid, Mid, Misere, Carlin, Palm, Pace Egg Day. The names Tid and Mid I cannot account for; Carlin Sunday was the day when carlins (small, hard black peas) were boiled and eaten. Mum did them sometimes but I did not find them very appetising.

Pace Egg Day was Easter Day. That was the day for children to have new clothes – the so-called 'pacey new'. Then you might go into white ankle socks for best instead of long woollen socks, but it depended on the weather. Eggs were prepared during the week preceding Easter Day, being hard-boiled and then dyed.

We gathered the yellow whin bloom for one colour, coffee grounds and onion peelings gave others. Sometimes either a pattern or initials were drawn on the egg with a candle before it was boiled. The candle wax did not take the dye, leaving the pattern in the natural colour of the eggshell when it was dyed. While the eggs were still warm, they were rubbed with buttered paper to give them a nice shine. Then they were given out to the children as presents on Easter Day. On Easter Monday, eggs were rolled down a slope until they cracked. They were also 'jarped', by which one child held his egg while another hit it with his egg. The winner was the one who kept his egg intact the longest. After all this, the 'remains' of the eggs were then eaten for tea with bread and butter. As only vegetable dyes were used, I assume they were harmless. I'm still here to tell the tale.

There were chocolate eggs at Easter. They were often hand made at Cairns in Berwick and other shops; not only chocolate but decorated with flowers made from icing. They also came in the shape of rabbits and other domestic animals. It seemed a shame to break and eat these lovely things and more than once I got into trouble for letting them go mouldy!

There was no Church in the valley, the nearest was that at Kirk–newton, parts of which are very old and contain the carvings thought in some quarters to represent the Three Wise Men who are wearing kilts. I do not know if anyone went down there, but we did have a Church service in the School once a month during the summer. There was none in winter as adverse weather conditions could make attendance difficult. Our services were inter–denominational, so it could be Rev. Maurice Piddocke from Kirknewton or the Presbyterian Minister who took the service. They were always held on Sunday afternoons after dinner and everybody attended. The shepherds brought their dogs who sat quietly under the chairs. After the service, the shepherds went straight out to 'look' their sheep.

Before the War, holidays were not generous. In the factories it was usual to have a weeks summer holiday. In Lancashire and Cheshire, my home since 1963, each town had its 'Wakes Week' when the population emigrated to Blackpool. No such thing in the valley. Risking constant repetition, this was sheep country and the sheep dont close down for 'Wakes Week'. They have to be looked after for 52 weeks. The residents, except us, did not go away on holiday. As we did not keep animals other than a goat and a few hens, we could go away, always to Mum's sister, Aunt Essie, who lived in Newcastle. We went there for a week or so in the summer school holidays. It was lucky for me as I could go to the seaside. I used to go to Whitley Bay and play on the beach or visit the 'Spanish City'. Uncle Jack took me down to the Quayside to the Sunday market there or to see the ships – he had been in the Merchant Navy.

The events which were of particular interest to the valley were the Agricultural Shows. Everybody went to the Wooler Show at the end of August. It was the event of the year when you met the rest of the farming community. Another of the big local Shows was the last of the season, the Alwinton Shepherds' Show in October. There were other Shows at Yetholm and Kirknewton, not so big as Wooler.

As well as the main events to select the best animals, the Shows have Domestic Sections. Shepherds have always been interested in and adept at stick dressing. They make carved heads for their sticks or crooks in a variety of designs, often using sheeps horns in a variety of ways, or depicting animals heads. They are works of art, done during the winter nights. The art of the wives and children was on show in the baking, handicrafts and painting sections where there was enthusiastic competition. I went to Wooler Show as a child and it has been a delight to visit some of these Shows again. Our nearest big Show is that at Bakewell in Derbyshire in August, but we did get to Wooler a couple of years ago and enjoyed it.

THE 3 Rs - DAYS AT SCHOOL.

It would have been nice to know something of the history of Southernknowe School. I tried to locate the school log books at Morpeth Record Office, but that for the period 1911 - 1953 was 'closed' and not available.

I also tried to find out who the teachers were by checking the Censuses held every 10 years. Those between 1861 and 1891, the most recent available, produced little information. Given that the school was opened in 1854 and must have had a teacher, it seemed logical to think that the teacher would reside not far from Southernknowe. In fact, the only person claiming to be a teacher appeared in the 1861 Census. She was a 17 year old girl called Barbara Bennett, born at Scremerston, and living at Trowburn with a shepherding family called Rutherford.

The opening date of 1854 is quoted by courtesy of the Glendale Local History Society. The school survived as such until 1968 when the remaining 6 children were transferred to Kirknewton School.

I did visit the school once not long before it closed and nothing much seemed to have changed since my time there. I think the teacher was expecting to take early retirement and move to Beckingham in Lincolnshire. The name in my mind was Miss Barker. She did not follow Mum, whose successors were Mrs.Norman and Mrs.North.

The school building itself seems to have been a one-roomed extension to Southernknowe Farmhouse, with Mrs.Cavers' living room and bedroom through the party wall.

Entry was first into a wooden porch which had coat hangars, space to store wellingtons or boots and a sink with cold water. From the porch you entered the single classroom which had the teacher's desk near the door and a coal fire on the gable end wall. On the same side as the porch was a window overlooking the farmyard, and opposite, two windows looking over the fields in the general direction of the Lambden Burn and Fleehope. Outside on the gable end wall was a coal/stickhouse.

The roll was never large − 6 on closure and about 9 in my time. There were two rows of desks, desks of different sizes bearing in mind that pupils were from 5 to 14 years of age. The bigger children sat in the row nearer the field view and the little ones had the view into the farmyard − where my eyes wandered often!.

Mum had a big old-fashioned desk with a cupboard underneath, and behind her on the wall was a row of cupboards holding all the books and equipment. Above these cupboards were several pictures. One was 'The Good Shepherd' which as a child I felt represented Mr.Cavers. Another was Holman Hunt's 'The Light of the World' and a third was one whose title I cannot recall but was of a little girl in a bluebell wood with rabbits nearby. Another was of St.Francis of Assisi, standing with outstretched arms, surrounded by birds and animals. There were others, too, including 'When did you last see your Father?' and the 'Laughing Cavalier' as well as pictures taken from the monthly magazines 'Child Education' and 'Pictorial Education' which Mum bought. What was coming in the new edition of each magazine was anticipated.

On one of the window sills was a Globe, much used.

As I have related, Mum took over the school in January 1929. Now I was too young to be a normal pupil but there was nobody to look after me so Mum took me to school with her and, I take it, the blessing of the Education Committee. So I started before nursery education was normal.

Looking back to the 1930s, it was another world. Children left school at 14 unless they took − and passed − the Scholarship at 11. If successful they had to go to school at Alnwick. That entailed the cost of lodgings, as well as school uniforms and other accoutrements which not everybody could afford. There was also the need for the boys to take up work on the farms, releasing the cost of a hired lad. I was fortunate in that I passed the Scholarship and I did go to the Duchess' School. Lodgings in Alnwick cost 10/- (50p) per week which Mum and Dad had to pay. To put that apparently paltry sum into context, my husband's parents had £2.00 per week income at that time for the family.

Compared with other places, there were some benefits in education at Southernknowe School as it had only a handful of pupils, each receiving far more personal attention than in the usual town classes of 30 or more.

So what was the school day like?.

Every morning started and every afternoon finished with prayers. At the end of the day we sang 'Now the day is over' and another I cannot recall in full. It began, 'Hands together, eyes shut tight.... and finished....cold as paddocks though they be, yet we hold them up to thee'. I would like to know what that was since the word 'paddock' is a local word for a toad and thus does not seem to fit into a hymn book for general use. Another favourite hymn was 'All things bright and beautiful' and that one I could never fathom out, 'We plough the fields and scatter'. Why ever and where to do you scatter having ploughed the fields? Now I realise that they sowed seed with a 'fiddle' in the past and the words were quite appropriate. The school had a harmonium which Mum played.

Having wandered off the order of the day, let me return to it.

After morning prayers there was always scripture; a bible story perhaps before settling in to learn the 3 'Rs'. Every morning without fail we had reading, writing and arithmetic with tests on them regularly. The infants started off writing with a slate and chalk, progressing to pencil and paper and eventually to pen and ink. That was with those old scratchy pen nibs and ink from the inkwells which blotted and got all over your fingers. The inkwells had to be washed out regularly at the cold tap in the porch and refilled, a job for one of the older boys.

You had to learn to write neatly and sometimes laboriously, making nice copperplate writing. As you got older, your writing would be to copy out a piece of poetry or prose. The older children helped when required by hearing the little ones read, so that Mum could be attending to a child at another level.

I had a favourite poem by James Hogg, the 'Ettrick Shepherd'.

It was the 'Boys Song':—

> 'Where the pools are bright and deep,
> Where the grey trout lies asleep,
> Up the river and o'er the lea,
> Thats the way for Billy and me.

'Where the blackbird sings the latest,
 Where the hawthorn blooms the sweetest,
 Where the nestlings chirp and flee,
 Thats the way for Billy and me.

'Where the mowers mow the cleanest,
 Where the hay lies thick and greenest,
 There to track the homeward bee,
 Thats the way for Billy and me.

'Where the hazel bank is steepest,
 Where the shadow falls the deepest,
 Where the clustering nuts fall free,
 Thats the way for Billy and me.

That poem epitomises for me all the feelings I had and still have for my childhood in the College Valley.

On a more mundane basis, times tables were up on the wall – and you learnt them – or else...!

As well as the 3Rs, we had History and Geography. Mum might make a history lesson from the picture 'When did you last see your Father'. but I did not find history absorbing and I preferred Geography. We had a cloth backed book with a yellow cover, it was 'Children of many Lands'. Now that was really interesting. It told you about the way of life of children from all over the World – what they wore, etc. We still have a copy of that book at home, its ownership always in contention with my husband. He used it too, but his memory is of a different part in which there is a large scale map of a town complete with tram lines and you had to describe the way home from school. Now he has spent his working life in transport and is a map enthusiast, so he would remember that!.

I almost forgot to add that there was a big school clock on the wall from which I learnt to tell the time.

By now it would be dinnertime. There were no school dinners. The children took sandwiches and in winter Mum would sometimes heat soup on the fire. The kettle had to be boiled on the fire too, and Mum made tea and cocoa. Cocoa was popular and with tins of Cadbury's Bournville Cocoa came lead models of Jonathan and the Cococubs, which I collected. These models would be quite collectable and valuable now – and illegal!

44

Southernknowe School c.1937. The children are the Little and Bertram families and me. The rugs are hand made with Paton's rug wool, cut into short lengths(thrums).

Southernknowe School c.1932. Mum, with Robert, Jimmy, and John Bertram; Ellen, Wattie,and Mabel Little, and me.

We had playtime, outside as much as possible, where we ran around and played with balls and skipping ropes. Both boys and girls played football using stones for rudimentary goalposts. There was no playground, we played in the field.

When the weather was wet we had to play inside for which Mum had a box of games – dominoes, draughts, jigsaws, etc. To have been kept in a single room all day must have been quite trying for the children, let alone the teacher.

Corporal punishment was allowed then and my husband remembers the British School at Berwick with Mr.Parker's cane and Miss Ferrell's strap only too well. Mum had a strap but I think she used it only once, and I am not disclosing the name of the recipient.

In the afternoons we had other lessons. I spoke earlier about my favourite poem by James Hogg, but we learnt many others. By Burns – Tam o'Shanter; by R.L.Stevenson; and another favourite poet, A.A.Milne. His poem, 'Daffodowndilly', was the first piece I taught my children at a very early age. We also had 'The Lady of Shallote' and some of the Border Ballads such as 'Young Lochinvar'. Christina Rossetti was another favoured, and I can still recall many of these poems now. As a teacher at West Lilburn and at East Ord I taught them to my pupils and later to my own children.

We had singing with Mum at the harmonium. I liked it but it was not universally popular especially with the boys. By 14, the boys' voices were breaking and it must have been uncomfortable and embarrassing for them. Mum could have been more thoughtful.

Art was another subject for the afternoon. Mum was not very good at Art and I doubt if it was successful, but one of my contemporaries, Ellen Little, was exceptionally good at it. We made calendars and cards at Christmas; at other times we might draw a wild flower or some sort of still life arrangement.

Seasonally there were always wild flowers in a vase on the window sill, and nature study was enjoyed. It came as second nature to the children. The changes in the seasons were watched.

For example, the arrival of the wheatears heralded the spring. We watched for the hazel catkins opening; we noted the so-called 'Peesweep storm', and listened for the call of the curlew or whaup as it was known there. It is an appropriate symbol for the Northumberland National Park. To some, an eerie cry: to me, a delight.

'Peesweep' is the local name for a peewit or lapwing, and the

'Peesweep storm' was always the last brief snowfall of the winter. It would be in late March or April or even later and would occur when the ground-nesting peewit was nesting and would suffer the consequences of the snowfall. Pesticides were not used. We knew where the wild creatures lived and they were respected. Dippers always lived on the burn; ravens nested in Hen Hole; butterwort grew in boggy places and all these represented the seasons. You looked for them and they provided a calendar of life.

It was not uncommon for someone to bring in a lizard or a newt or some tadpoles. Dad's brother, Uncle Norman, was a Merchant Navy Officer. He brought us an armadillo shell plus various large shells he collected on his travels and they were kept in the school. At some time, somebody — I think a visitor to Coldburn — had caught an adder and had it preserved in spirit in a jam jar. The jar stood on the window sill for all to see so as to recognise an adder. They are not uncommon in the Cheviots and can give a nasty bite. I was brought up to be very wary of these creatures which, whilst timid and will try to hide away, are not easily seen when basking in the sunshine. It was brought home to me a couple of years ago when a friend got out of a car at Wooler Common, and having unwittingly stood on one, received a severe bite. There was no serum at Wooler, nor at Berwick, nor at the RVI at Newcastle, and some was eventually flown from London but not before the poison had swollen her leg and reached her body. She was ill for many months after it and her leg has never returned to normal.

I should not wish to put any priority on lessons, but one thing we did get importantly was handwork.

Everybody was taught the rudiments of knitting and sewing. All the boys could darn a sock, mend a tear, and sew on a button before they left school. Since it was not uncommon for them to leave home to become hired lads at nearby farms, it was vital that they could do these things. The shepherds or farmers wives had no time to do these jobs for them.

The first thing to be knitted was always a kettle holder. The next was usually a scarf and they moved on to knit gloves and socks and all could knit a sock and turn a heel.

The girls made garments, all hand sewn; things like aprons, for which Mum got the material from the travelling draper, or some may have come with the requisition made to the education authority. We also did weaving. The infants started weaving using squares of cardboard with serrated edges as if cut with pinking shears. You wound the wool first up and down the cards, putting it into each serration, and then you made the warp (or weft?) by darning the wool lengthways along the card. Finally the card was removed and the result was a teapot stand. Quite recently I was speaking to a well-known Wooler man, Andy Fairnington, whose elder brother was Jack, the Glendale Co-op driver. He described making that type of teapot stand. He also made a ball which was stuffed with sheeps wool. I have to digress and report a little more of my conversation with him. He went to school in Wooler. There he was taught to scrub a floor, polish a floor, and clean windows properly, and he emphasised properly!. He added that Mum had taught him to sew when he stayed at Coldburn, adding that it put him in good stead in the Army.

Mum bought some small weaving looms in which the cardboard squares were replaced by celluloid pieces which could be moved to allow the use of different coloured wools.

I mentioned earlier that 'clooty' mats were made. Mum moved a bit 'up-market' and introduced wool rugs, using rug wool bought from Patons. It came in big hanks which had to be wound and cut into short equal lengths using a thrum stick. That was hard work and sore on the hands. We made two for our own house when we were married and keep two of those original wool rugs from Coldburn as well as a photo of the Southernknowe children holding up a completed rug outside the school.

I have written a lot about handwork, but it was not done every day. After all these years, it is not possible to recall the proportion of time spent on any particular thing, rather I have documented what comes to my mind. It is a pity the school log books have gone.

Like every other school, we had periodic visits from Inspectors, and there was always trepidation in case they asked you a question. Some of them seemed quite friendly.

There was a visitation from the School Nurse once in a blue moon. She used to tell you to show your hands. You were made to strip to the waist for her to examine you, and as mothers came, that would be by appointment. The children had to go outside, returning to the classroom one at a time for the dreaded examination. I never recall any problems – the children were generally fit as far as I know.

A School Doctor also came, of whom I remember nothing. I imagine it was an annual visit.

There was also the School Dentist. I remember him because he gave me a lift in his car – my first car ride. The car would be an old bullnose Morris or the like, complete with 'dicky seat'. He opened this seat and took me to Coldburn and the Bertram lads to Dunsdale. I do not know what he did professionally as he had no equipment with him. He may have sent some to the dentist in Wooler, but I never had any dental treatment until I was an adult and I have my own teeth, long since subject to regular checks. Maybe the diet in the valley reduced the incidence of decay. We did not eat a lot of sweets; we drank a lot of milk for calcium and we cleaned our teeth. On that score Mum was keen on cleaning teeth. I am sure everybody had toothbrushes and my contemporaries will not need to be reminded of Gibbs' Dentifrice and 'Ivory Castles'.

Mum's job was not quite what teachers might expect nowadays. Of course she did the teaching, and she looked after the 'school meal service' as I have mentioned, but she was also the school cleaner.

Jessie Cavers, from the farm, had the school key and went in early in the morning to light the fire. For that, the older boys had to bring in coal and sticks before they went home.

Once the children had gone, Mum had to clean out the fireplace and sweep the school clean. She had to clean the windows and once a week she had to scrub the floor. While she did that I went to Jessie Cavers for my blackcurrant tart and to help her with the various jobs I have already mentioned.

I liked to be home by 5 o'clock. That was time for 'Childrens' Hour' with Uncle Mac on the radio. I wonder how many remember Toytown with Larry the Lamb, Mr.Grouser, and the rest of them. That was my favourite radio programme. We got no homework, hardly surprising as some children had to walk a couple of miles and had to do their jobs when they got home.

So that was school – how different from today – another world!.

THE CAVERS FAMILY.

I picked out the Cavers family at Southernknowe Farm because they were our closest neighbours and I did a lot with them. They were special friends whom I have never forgotten.

They were our first contacts in the valley and their house is where we spent our first night in the new environment. The kindness and hospitality we received from them must have started us out on the happy footing we had at Coldburn.

Southernknowe Farm was at that time owned by Mr.Cavers, and not tenanted as were most of the other houses. When we arrived, Mr.and Mrs.Cavers would be about 75 years old, and the farm was run by their son, Anthony (Anty), and his wife, Jessie Scott. Anty would then be 39. He and Jessie had no children and in some respects I was the nearest to that role for them. As well as Anthony, there were two daughters, Janet and Phemie, both civil servants in London, returning to the valley for holidays.

Mr.James Cavers died in 1933 and right to the last he took an active part in the work of the farm. He had come from Scotland, I think from around Eccles in Berwickshire, but Mrs.Cavers was born in Elsdon, Northumberland. They were well into their 30s before they had their family. Looking at the 1891 Census – the most recent available to the public – I saw that the two older children, one of whom must have died young, were born in Scotland, while the two younger were born in Kirknewton Parish. In that year, 1891, Mr.Cavers was a shepherd at Mounthooly. When we knew him he had bought Southernknowe. His daughters were civil servants and he must have had to pay for their education. Now to do those things on a shepherd's wage was no mean feat. They had had to be very thrifty to ensure that their daughters had jobs and their son his own farm. It brings into perspective the materialism of today. They were not a mean family, indeed they were very kind We used to get tramps coming up the valley, regulars who came up to earn a little by doing odd jobs. One, whose name I have forgotten, came to Southernknowe and always got work. He slept in the barn but was forbidden to light his pipe. The family were well respected locally and unlike the shepherds who always used first names, the Cavers were always 'Mr.' and 'Mrs'.

Anthony Cavers was an athletic man, a fell runner, who developed heart trouble. In his latter days he was unable to climb hills to look

Cavers family c.1932.

Anthony (left) and Gordon.

Southernknowe. The far building contained the house at
the far end, with the big porch, and the school occupies
the nearer end. Part of a haystack is in the yard, and
a hay 'pike' is beyond the house.

after the animals and had to resort to horseback. He died in 1939 aged 49, and with his father, is buried in Kirknewton Churchyard. After Anthony's death, Jessie and Mrs.Cavers left the valley, moving back to the Belses area, from which I understood Jessie came. Mrs.Cavers died at Belses in 1950 aged 98, and Jessie moved to Penrith with her brother. We kept in touch with her up to her death at Renwick in 1975.

As they had no family, they always had a hired lad. I remember them but I cannot recall any of their names now. They converted the loft into two rooms, one leading off the other, and the hired lads slept there.

The Cavers' brought up and trained a foxhound pup. They received it when it was weaned, at about two months old, and trained it on behalf of the College Valley Hunt. It was returned there when trained and old enough to run with the pack. This was a continuous process, with each pup being replaced by another.

Mr.Cavers used to wear a shepherd tartan plaid, the only man in the area to do so. Mrs.Cavers always wore black, a long black skirt down to her ankles and a black apron. Her hair was tied in a bun and I have a lovely photo of them in dress more Victorian than of the 1930s. After all, she was born in 1852. The family were the essence of gentleness – they were the kindest of people.

My memories of their house are remarkably clear. The school was an extension on to one end of Southernknowe Farm. The farmhouse itself was entered by a flagged porch sited at the opposite gable end to the school. In the porch was a sink and tap and a copper boiler as it served as Jessie's washhouse too. As well as a place to keep boots and outdoor clothing, there was a table or bench in one corner. From the porch there was a door into a vestibule, from which the stairs went up to the left. Straight ahead was a door into the 'best' bedroom. On the right was the living room. I am not sure if it, too, had a stone floor. In common with the other houses, there was a big table in front of the window and behind it and below the window was a long wooden bench. When not in use, the table had a chenille tablecloth with a fringe. At each end of the table was a wooden chair, one for Mr.Cavers and the other for Anthony. Facing the window were two chairs for the two wives. Children sat at the bench below the window, as did the hired lad. At the other end of the room was a black range with a chair at each side of it. At one side was a rocking chair and at the other a wooden chair with a very high back and wings to keep out the draughts. They had cushions, hand crocheted, and Otterburn rugs to keep your back warm. 'Stocking Willie' used to sell these rugs. Off here was the door into Jessie and Anthony's bedroom.

On the other side of the living room was a box bed built into the wall. It was curtained off for use by Mr. and Mrs.Cavers. None of the other houses in the valley had a box bed so Southernknowe must have been one of the oldest properties. There were no easy chairs as such. Mrs.Cavers usually had the rocking chair, and the other one was a real museum piece possibly handed down through the Cavers family. I cannot recall whether or not they had a paraffin stove in addition to the coal range. It was in this room that I used to sit as a child and where Mrs.Cavers taught me rhymes and poetry. She taught me many of the traditional songs – 'C'a the yowes tae the knowes', etc. She liked me to sing to her. I never knew my Granny Dent and rarely saw Granny Cowe, so Mrs.Cavers was a substitute 'Granny' for me.

As I have related elsewhere, I went to Cavers' after school every day while Mum finished her work in the school. It was there that Jessie, too, did so much for me, teaching me to milk cows, make butter, and generally help to give me a memorable childhood.

The men were usually out when I was there after school so I saw less of them but I still knew them well and knew them as quiet and gentle people. One thing does remain in my mind – on Sunday the only work allowed was seeing to the animals and cooking dinner. All papers and books were put away except for the Bible and the 'Peoples' Friend' which were left on the table.

Apart from my after school visits, I went to tea with the family sometimes. Meals were always preceded by Grace, said by Mr.Cavers, and followed by a prayer of thanks – 'For what we have received, may the Lord make us truly thankful, Amen'. After Mr.Cavers' death, Anthony continued to do this.

ANOTHER NOTABLE – MISS PEASE.

Miss Ella Pease was not a permanent resident of College Valley, but had a holiday bungalow there and took a great interest in it. All I know of her background is that she came from a shipping or engineering family – a Quaker family – and that she lived in a big house on the sea front at Alnmouth. I do not think she had any relatives. The house at Alnmouth, Nether Grange, is now a holiday house owned by the Holiday Fellowship, catering for about 60 guests and offering a programme of walking holidays in Northumberland. Their walks include the College Valley and the Cheviot area and they also offer holidays with a specialist programme on the history of the area. It seems a most fitting use following her interest in the valley. How and when she started coming to the valley I do not know, but by the time we arrived there she had a small wooden bungalow built just above the valley road near Whitehall. It is approached by a grass track over a field and it stands today apparently unaltered except for a TV aerial. I think she just took a liking to the valley and came up for summer holidays and at Christmas, with odd visits in between.

She came up by car for which she had a chauffeur, and with a ladysmaid. I have them on photo but I have forgotten their names. They may have been husband and wife as they accompanied her always doing cooking, cleaning, etc., when they were there. To me as a child, she seemed to be an old lady, but with hindsight, she was probably not so old at all. She was a lovely person – a real lady – well respected by everybody.

She had travelled abroad widely – to India and China, for instance. She gave me a number of small items she had acquired, all of which we still have. They include a cup and saucer from China; a set of Russian dolls which fit inside one another; and a tiny elephant, carved from ivory and small enough to fit inside a seed. She had stopped on the roadside somewhere in India and seen this being carved, and bought it.

She took a great interest in the school and always referred to it as 'her' school. She visited it quite often, so I saw quite a lot of her and Mum enjoyed a good and friendly relationship with her.

There is one particular occasion especially remembered, and that was in 1930, on the last day of the passenger train service to Kirknewton.

She invited the children and their mothers to her house at Alnmouth for tea. We all went down to Kirknewton Station by horse and cart and duly caught the train to Alnwick. For all or most of the children it was their first train journey, and for some, their first visit to the seaside. Since the children normally wore boots, which were not quite right for the occasion, on arrival at Alnwick, we

54

A school picnic with Miss Pease(third from left), her ladysmaid, and chauffeur at her bungalow in College Valley, c.1934.

The school outing to Nether Grange, Alnmouth to visit Miss Pease in August 1930. Note the boys' 'Sunday best'.

went to a shoe shop to buy sandshoes for the children. The shop was on Clayport and had two rooms, one behind the other; the back room containing the childrens footwear. Here the shopkeeper had to switch on the electric light, much to the incredulity of the children who had never seen it before. Mum had to stop the boys from switching it on and off. We got our sandshoes and carried on to Alnmouth. At Nether Grange, Miss Pease had tea set out on a lovely china tea set in a big room whose french windows were open to the garden. I had to go with Mum and sit quietly to take tea with Miss Pease there. This was much to my chagrin as the other children were out on the lawn playing, and they were each given a paper bag with sandwiches and cake. I was jealous!.

After tea we went across to the beach to play there – and I have another photo of the gathered throng in their Sunday best, with the boys wearing the big caps of the day. Now the children were used to playing in the burn, and there are no waves on the burn. When they went into the sea, they were surprised when the first waves came in and the Bertram boys promptly sat down in the water, fully clothed. Despite that, we all had a lovely time. The return journey to Kirknewton was on the very last passenger train on that line, and I remember the bangs of detonators, usually put on by signalmen to alert drivers to signals in foggy weather. They were to commemorate the demise of the service.

That trip to Alnmouth was never repeated, most probably because of transport difficulties, but we were entertained by Miss Pease on other occasions. We had picnics in the field at her bungalow and I have another photo taken at one of these and on which Miss Pease and her chaffeur and ladysmaid appear with the children.

At Christmas when we had a party, she always brought a big box or jar of sweets to the school. I recollect Horner's 'Dainty Dinah' toffees being brought. We sorted them into the various kinds and shared them out.

So she left me with a happy memory.

STRANGERS ABOUND.

Despite its remoteness, College Valley had quite a lot of visitors. They enjoyed its tranquillity and the opportunities for walking and for climbing Cheviot.

Mum was a very sociable person and many if not all of the regular visitors either called on us or stayed with us at Coldburn.

We have many old photos, not of very good quality, and using these, I have managed to list some of the visitors.

The Scouts from Berwick were very frequent visitors and some continued to come after they left the Rover Scouts. Most of the photos show them wearing kilts. The two who immediately come to my mind were Tom Fraser, whose father had the saddlers in Hide Hill, Berwick, and a lad called Erskine, whose christian name escapes me. Barney Parkes also appears with them. The Scouts had a hut at Fleehope and came to Coldburn from there.

Mum's interest in scouting went back a long time. In her teens, she had joined the organisation as one of the early Girl Boy Scouts, the forerunner of the Girl Guide movement. She received a medal from the Royal Humane Society for her part in the rescue of a boy from the River Wear at Durham, where she was then living. In recognition of her help to the Berwick Scouts, they recommended that she receive a 'Thanks Badge', which we retain in the family.

From the Newcastle area we had many visitors, and apart from Fred Heward, whose father had worked as a young joiner with Dad at Galashons, I do not know how we came to be in touch with them. Fred Heward brought a friend, Tommy Hooker, not a joiner, but from Horner's 'Dainty Dinah' works at Chester-le-Street.

We had a botanist from Newcastle who brought his assistant. Their names are forgotten, but not their excitement at finding a rare plant on Cheviot, and hearing them talking about Stagshorn Moss and Cloudberries, the latter found only at a high level.

Another who stayed with us was a Geologist. He was Indian with a name I can only remember as abbreviated by us to 'Jingy'. He too came from Newcastle University, and either he or a colleague studied the ancient British Camps to be found all over the area. Staying at Coldburn, he demonstrated some Indian recipes. One still familiar is the so-called 'Jingy' pudding. It was made by melting butter in a pan, adding semolina, then milk, sweetening to taste. I have not written the recipe down so there may be a missing ingredient. The proper thing was delicious but rich. He made curries but they were not to my taste.

We had a medical student, 'Tax' Cockburn, who came from Tyneside with his sister, Irene. They were walkers. He graduated to become a Doctor while we were there. He was Thomas Aidan Cockburn, to give him his full name.

Geologists from India via Newcastle University c.1938
Mr.'Jingy'(left) and his colleague with us on Raingauge
Hill, Coldburn, our Weather Station.

More visitors from Newcastle University. In the
centre are the Botanist and his Assistant. On the
School wall is the old 'County Library' sign.

Also from Tyneside was a teacher, Edith Wilson (later Mrs.Hugh Jackson from Low Fell). She,too, had a sister, Sadie. They were frequent visitors and Mum always kept in touch with them.

It was something of a 'Mecca' for motor cyclists. A regular group were Harry Meadows, and twin brothers, Rix and Maurice Duncan, the latter from Cullercoats; as well as cousins, Ray Niven and Ron Hall. Rix and Maurice came up for years until they were both called up early in the war. They had new twin motor bikes with consecutive registration numbers for their 21st birthdays. Maurice was to become an Army dispatch rider and, sadly, he was killed quite early in the war. Rix was also in the army, but he returned to Cullercoats and married Phyllis, who also visited us. Harry Meadows joined the Navy, moving to London after the war.

In fact we had quite a hectic social life with visitors as well as with the valley people. The visitors came summer and winter and Dad used to bike with them. Winter visits were sometimes coloured by someone coming off their bike into the snow, and we have a photo of a visitor's car that had come off the road and had to be pulled out. In due course, my sister, Winnie, got a motor bike. Had we stayed there, I might have had one too, but I was too young. Reading this, the reaction of my family was 'it was alright for you, but you wouldnt let us have bikes!'. Stockport's traffic was not quite that of the College Valley in those days.

TODDLER TO TEENAGER.

My home was in the valley from 1929 until 1941, but in September 1938, having passed the 'Scholarship', I had to leave Southernknowe School and go to the nearest Grammar School, which was the Duchess' School in Alnwick. It was far too far to travel daily, so for three years, I lodged in Alnwick to go to school, returning home to Coldburn at weekends. Our departure from Coldburn in 1941 was not entirely voluntary. Dad was too old for the Army, but he was directed into war work at Allan Bros. in Tweedmouth – 'the Woodyard' – so we had to move.

I had had three sisters, Winnie, Connie and Dorothy. I never knew the latter two. Connie died of scarlet fever in 1919, only weeks after Mum lost both her parents in the dreadful 'flu epidemic of that year which killed millions world-wide. Dorothy died at Belford

Moor when I was a few months old, and Winnie, the eldest, was much older than me. Winnie left home when I was very young to train at Newton Rigg College, Penrith, and having completed that successfully, she took charge of the dairy at Whittingham Hospital, Preston, Lancs. It had its own farms and she looked after the making of butter and cheese for the hospital as well as general dairying matters.

Thus I was more or less an only child at Coldburn, but it did not mean I was a lonely child. Of course there were times when I had to play alone and I had for a companion my Teddy. Now Teddy was a friend and I treated him as if he were a person. I did not like him to have big ears so I removed them. Every time Mum put them back I took them off. He never went without clothes. He had a jacket knitted by Mrs.Cavers. Apart from sewing on the ears, Mum and Jessie went along with me and treated him as a person. Now I loved plodging in the burn, so somewhere or other, Jessie found a tiny pair of wellingtons, a raincoat, and a sou'wester to fit Teddy, and when I went plodging, Teddy went, too.

I dont know where he came from. I suppose Mum and Dad bought him when I was very small as I took him up the valley from Belford. He was put away safely in a box as many adults do, reluctant to part with favourite toys and he is in our boxroom. I was tempted to cremate him not so long ago, but then I visited the Museum of Childhood at Ribchester in Lancashire. Seeing there so many beloved Teddies, I felt he must go there. Then I read that the Museum was to be closed, so he remains in the boxroom.

Dad made a large rocking elephant for me when we first moved to Coldburn. I could not say 'elephant' and he acquired the name 'Heffalump'. I spent many happy hours with him but he escaped the net and was given away when outgrown. Dad also made dolls furniture and a dolls cradle for me. They were beautifully made – much larger than average – and again they were things much cherished. If it was fine, they would be taken out into the field to play houses. I used stones to make the ground plan of a house with several rooms, and a gap in the dry stone wall in the field was the fireplace. I had small pans into which I put nettle or dock leaves to make pretend soup. These plants grow together and one makes an antidote for the other, but you can pick nettles carefully and not get stung. As with Teddy, we still have the dolls furniture stored in the boxroom and it really ought to go into a museum.

It was common to have a Noah's Ark, another of Dad's handiworks together with wooden farm animals plus whatever I added from the 'Cococubs' given free with Cadbury's cocoa. I was very, very lucky to have a father capable and willing to make these toys for me, and in return, they were cared for. How many are there like that nowadays?. I see hand—made wooden toys at craft fairs, costing a fortune, but made with the same loving care.

For winter, I had a sledge for 2, and 2 toboggans, one small, the other big enough for 6, all home—made.

At the risk of incurring wrath in some quarters, I have to add that I had a golliwog. It is sad that one hardly dare mention the word nowadays. At that time, gollies were universally enjoyed, and our Indian friend, 'Jingy', never took exception to my golly.

What may not be appreciated is that they were a country craft and most mothers made their children gollies from old black stockings — black stockings being normal everyday wear. It was another way of using up old material at a time when money for toys was just not available. Pegs were also dressed as dolls. Having had these things has not made me racially prejudiced. Concurrent with the offending golly, I was enthusiastic to learn about children from other lands at school. It is all very sad.

Apart from Southernknowe Farm which was not far away, we had no near neighbours, so as a small child I could not wander off to other houses to play. I did have to go up to Dunsdale for milk sometimes, giving a chance to play football with the Bertram boys or later play with the Dagg family.

I had a bike too, but used it to play only locally and only when I got a bit older would I go with Belle or Margaret Dagg down maybe to Hethpool, but no further. That would change when I was 11.

Mum kept hens and a pedigree white goat, Prue. We got her from Kirknewton soon after we moved into Coldburn and I remember leading her up from there late one evening. Prue used to wander about nearby on Coldburn Hill, coming back to the byre at night. Once she wandered off a bit too far and mated with one of the wild goats which roam the valley. She produced 2 kids — a white billy and a brown and white nanny. We kept Peggy, the nanny, but the billy was sold to the College Valley Hunt to get the hounds used to goats thus avoiding their chasing the wild ones. We used the goats milk for drinking but there was never enough to justify cheese making. Prue was sold to somebody at Ponteland before I went to Alnwick; Peggy died after I went there.

For a short time in early days, we had fantail pigeons. They did not stay long and I have no idea why we had them at all. We also had angora rabbits. They were well looked after and their lovely coats brushed regularly. Mum may have had the idea of selling the fur but we never had enough to do so. They were happy to be handled but one wandered off and mated with a wild rabbit. Her brood were not tame at all and would not be picked up. They were released into the wild.

We always had a dog, a Border terrier, Vicky. She lived to a good age, surviving until we were in Berwick. There was also a Manx cat, Mons. She lived to be 13, producing many kittens and was buried on Coldburn Hill. You had to have cats to keep rodents at bay. When we had to move to Berwick, there was no possibility of taking country cats into the town nor could they be left to wander and go wild. Dad had to do something about it. He loaded his gun, put down a saucer of milk, and destroyed them with a single shot.

Thinking about guns causes me to digress. From time to time the valley was troubled with tinkers who helped themselves to hens, etc., and generally made themselves a nuisance. One day Mum heard they were in the valley and, knowing that Winnie was alone at Coldburn, sent one of the boys from school across the fields to Coldburn to alert her. Now Winnie had learnt how to handle a gun. When the offending visitors arrived, she came out of the house, loaded the gun in front of them and told them she could use it – and to go away. To prove the point, she fired a shot over their heads. They departed down the valley at speed and never came back in our time.

I enjoyed climbing trees and had various episodes of torn clothing. Another episode, when I would be getting a bit older, involved Belle Dagg. We were playing at Coldburn and Cavers' carthorse, Prince, was there on Coldburn Hill, grazing. We thought we would like to ride it, so, without a saddle, the two of us got on its back, Belle at the front holding its mane, while I held on to Belle's waist. Prince was not amused and galloped off up Coldburn Hill. With nothing to hold on to, I slid gently off its back, followed by Belle and landed in the bracken without harm.

Like Dad I have always enjoyed making things. I enjoyed drawing and painting but I also helped him with jobs. When he was doing joinery, I had bring tools and sort nails and screws. With the motor bike I learnt how to clean sparking plugs. It was all part of the culture of self sufficiency one had to learn living there.

When the bike had been done, I often went with him as a pillion passenger – no helmets then. We might have a run to Chatton or Lowick to test the bike. One Sunday we had been doing the bike and he told Mum we were going for a run. At Kirknewton he asked me where I would like to go. I said 'the seaside', so off we went to Spittal. Now both of us had working things on and we were as black as sweeps. So much so that we dare not go on to the beach and we had to go on to the cliffs towards Cocklawburn. We were away for ages and Mum played war when we returned!.

STILL EN ROUTE FROM TODDLER TO TEENAGER.

One activity I enjoyed was haymaking. Strictly speaking this should have been included in the piece about the Daily Grind as it was a major seasonal task that fell on every inhabitant. Although I was the schoolteacher's daughter with nothing to do with the farms, every pair of hands was needed at hay time – however young – and it was a time of extra hard work for the women who had to take part and still do the cooking, milking, butter making and the usual jobs. There is no truer adage than 'make hay while the sun shines'. I used to help the Cavers family at Southernknowe when school was finished. Hay was cut in June so it was the school term. Remember that Jimmy Bertram never lost a days schooling, so he had to help after school.

As I recall, the hay was cut in swathes by reaper. It had to be dried thoroughly or it would rot so it had to be turned regularly by hand, using wide wooden rakes. The loss of the hay crop was a disaster so the women had to be out during the day turning it. Once dry there was great urgency to get it led in. First of all the lines of hay were gathered into heaps – there might have been a name for them – I dont remember. These heaps were then stacked carefully by hand into 'pikes' ready for leading in. They used a long narrow wooden bogie, longer than the usual cart, with only one axle and pulled by the carthorse. At the front of the bogie was a roller attached to a chain and a hand operated winch. The bogie was backed up to the pike and the back of it released, tipping it up. The chain was put round the bottom of the pike and kicked into it carefully. The chain was then winched up, pulling the pike on to the centre of the bogie, and levelling it. The bogie was then locked level and the pike secured with ropes. The making of the pike is a skilled job as it had to remain intact in loading, conveyance and unloading. My job was first to help Jessie turn the hay. Once the pikes were made, I was allowed to lead them in from the field to the stackyard. You stood on the front of the bogie, leaning back on the pike and holding the reins. Now I thought I was really useful doing a job like this. Little did I realise that Prince knew exactly what to do and did not need me to lead him. Anthony Cavers was in the field and Jessie and the hired lad in the stackyard. They unloaded, making either a stack, or if there was space in the barn, loading it there. As the haystack grew higher, then the hired lad went on top and Jessie had to pass up the hay by fork. It was very tiring for them. I then led Prince back to the field. The fact that I could lead the cart was very useful to the Cavers, even if only to allow Anthony a few minutes break. All the children contributed in some way to the haymaking even if only to bring flasks of tea and previously made sandwiches from home to the field. There was no time for the men to go home so they had their 'piece' where they were. Cavers' hayfield was at Coldburn, half a mile from the farm and with gates to be opened and shut en route. Mum used to 'co-operate'. When she knew the empty bogie was going back from Southernknowe to Coldburn, she used to let the children out. They got a ride to Coldburn, and the Bertrams got home to Dunsdale a bit quicker! All this was part of the way of life established at an early age. The cows know when to come in; they gather in-bye and you know to bring them in. I would be doing these jobs when I was 8 or 9 years old and thought it was normal.

Eventually the time came for me to leave Southernknowe School. In those days – the 1930s – there was not a lot of scope for higher education. You could, at 11, take the so-called 'Scholarship', a predecessor of the 11+. If you were fortunate enough to pass, then you went on to Grammar School. From College Valley and Wooler, that was to the Duke's or Duchess' Schools at Alnwick. The other Grammar School was at Berwick. I did pass the Scholarship and went to Alnwick. Now I cannot think how many were in my year.

My husband passed for Berwick Grammar School, and the total intake in his year, male and female as it was then a mixed school was around 30. That was for Berwick town and the country area out almost to Wooler and Belford. Failing the Scholarship meant leaving school at 14. I think it is important to realise that at Southernknowe there was only a handful of pupils, allowing for a high degree of personal attention. Classes in town schools were larger and the level of personal tuition that much lower so we were lucky to go there.

Moving to Alnwick was a new life. Classes were totally different. But this is not relevant to life in the valley so I will not dwell on it, except to make another digression. By 1939 I had settled into the Duchess' School. Those were the days when everybody went to the pictures and Shirley Temple was the great child star. But the War had started too, and evacuees came to Alnwick from Newcastle. This day a new girl appeared in our class. She was small and neat with beautiful auburn/ginger curls. She carried a little attache case with the initials 'S.T.' She sat down beside me and the class started to whisper 'is it Shirley Temple?'; ask her her name, is it Shirley Temple?'. Well of course it was not the 'star' herself, but Sheila Temple from Newcastle. Sheila and I became friends and we still phone and visit each other.

So much for the digression. The move to Alnwick in September 1938 was a major change to my life even if it was not a culture shock. The valley was a community and you learnt to mix and to understand one another and I had no trouble settling in at Alnwick.

There was no special school transport and the nearest bus to Alnwick was Service 70 from Wooler at 0750. Given that children from Milfield to Berwick Grammar School had a daily taxi, I do not know why the different arrangement applied for Alnwick which had several boarders. It is 11 miles by road from Coldburn to Wooler. On Monday mornings, I had to be up by 0600, cycle the 11 miles via Hethpool, Kirknewton and Akeld to Wooler. There I left my bike at Atkinson's Garage and caught the bus which took an hour to reach Alnwick. There was no question of sleeping in – that was the one and only bus.

At Alnwick I lodged with Mrs.Ferguson in Chapel Lane, along with two other pupils, Annie Dunlop, a senior girl from Budle; and

Doreen Thompson, whose father was a shepherd in the Ingram Valley. Doreen moved later to Felton. They were happy days and Mrs.Ferguson was a lovely person who gave us a 'real' home with her own family, Mary, Alice and Jimmy. We continued to visit Mrs.Ferguson after we were married and until we left the area.

We could go back to Coldburn on Friday night on the 4 o'clock bus from Alnwick, with a repeat performance, collecting the bike from Atkinsons and cycling back home. Since Dad worked away from home, it meant that sometimes he would take me to and from Alnwick on the back of his motor bike but that had to be planned carefully in advance. Also, were I to go home on his motor bike, I had to go to the butchers in Clayport and collect a piece of sirloin for the Sunday dinner.

Cycling was OK during the summer but not in winter. Then Dad took me to Wooler on the motor bike on Sunday evening to catch the 7 o'clock bus to Alnwick and I came back from Alnwick on Saturday morning. If the weather was really bad and the roads blocked, then I just had to stay with Mrs.Ferguson. The winter of 1940 was very severe and I must have been away from Coldburn for some time. 1940 was also the blackout and when I went with Dad on the motor bike, all he had for lighting on the bike was a lamp, shielded, and with only a narrow strip of light showing. It did not make the journey over the rough valley road either easy or rapid.

So that was my College Valley childhood. It was a wonderful time and I am ever grateful that it happened in the way it did.

Life was not always games. We had a garden in which I loved to work. I grew vegetables and loved flowers and learnt the wild flowers. Now we have nearly an acre of town garden and my love of gardening has never died. Nor has my gratitude that life has allowed me to visit and enjoy lovely gardens nationwide – Wisley; Ness Gardens in the Wirral; Harlow Car Gardens at Harrogate and so many others.

Both Mum and Jessie taught me to cook. I learnt all the traditional things like scones, girdle scones and fruit cakes. These have I passed on to my family who know these traditions must be maintained. Our diet is broader now and not only do we travel in Europe, but we receive many visitors from there. No foreign visitor leaves without having tasted scones, home made jam and shortbread – made, of course, with butter.

My life has changed drastically over the years, but many of the habits and traditions learnt all those years ago in the College Valley die hard and I would not wish them to change.

As I have said earlier, the seasons governed daily life in the valley. The winter was not over until we had the 'Peesweep storm'. We watched for the wheatears and stonechats; we watched for the yellow whin bloom and for the dippers nesting under the bridge at Dunsdale. Nothing of that has changed – we see them if we return at the right season.

My love of the countryside, nurtured up there, has been passed on ; first to my husband, who came from Berwick and liked the sea; and to my family, all of whom love nature, love the country and love walking. For an appropriate celebration of our Ruby Wedding in 1991, three generations gathered in the Lake District to climb Helvellyn together. Weeks later we went up to do a circular walk from Cocklawfoot up to the Border Fence and round Auchope Rig. It was marvellous – long may it continue. Thank you, College!.

CONCLUDING – A LITTLE BIT OF HISTORY.

The name 'College', often appearing as 'Colledge' in old documents comes from the Anglo-Saxon 'col' and 'leche' meaning a bog or stream flowing through boggy land.

The earliest record I found referred to 'the free forest of Chyviot' in 1182 belonging to Thomas Muschamp of the Barony of Wooler. By the 13th century it had been divided into two 'moeties', the northern part on the English side known as Strangeways, and the southern section as Conyers. The dividing line appears to have been carefully marked in early charters but it is less easy to follow those lines today. The two sections were to become the 'Grey's Forest' and the 'Selby's Forest' of later days.

The most important early records of the Eastern Borders date from 1542–1550 and are known as Bowes Surveys and Reports. These Surveys were written by Sir Robert Bowes at the request of the Lord Marquis Dorsett, the Warden General. They contain complete reports on the state of the country, buildings, fords, etc, and land-owners on the south side of the Tweed. In 1542 Bowes gives a 'description of the Forest of Cheviot being parcel of the said East Marches'. It mentions 'a little river called Colledge' and another 'brook or water called Cawdgate'. 'The Forest of Cheviot is a mountain or great hill four miles or more of length lying between the head of Halterburn and the White Swire eastwards and the Hanging Stone westwards. Half of the Forest of Cheviot is of the inheritance of Lord Conyers and the other the inheritance of Sir James Strangeways Knight, deceased'.

State Papers of Henry 8th for 1543 refer in some detail to the College Valley area and in particular to the roads traversing it. They include 'the watter of College from Bowbent (Bowmont?) to the Hanging Stone; to the Wackridge Way; to Dowsons Rodde which comes over College Water 1½ miles above Hethpole; to the Cawdburne(Coldburn?) Rodde which goes over College Water at Sothoronlawe 3 miles above Hethpole; also the Hunt Rodde which goes over College Water at Plantengrene near Sothoronlawe and goes up Fleup: and to 'the busiest way of all' which comes down Preston Swyre and down Lambden Water and over College Water at the Hollinge Bush, 5 miles above Hethpole and enters Scotland at the Cribhede; Smalden Rodde and Roughside Rodde.' At least some of those are recognisable now.

Part of the Cheviot Forest was sold to Sir Ralph Grey in 1611. The sale document mentions various places including Hethpole, Trowup, Fleup,etc. and others long since gone, but not Southernknowe. Hence the name of the Parish of Grey's Forest. Dunsdale and Goldscleugh did not appear in any of the documents, but they came into Selby's Forest.

Daniel Defoe climbed Cheviot in his day. The weather must have been clear as he claimed to see Berwick, the smoke from the salt pans at Shields, and Soutra.

Tithes were referred to in the text. The word comes from Old English meaning one tenth part. It is a practice of great age, adopted by the Christian Church whereby people paid a tenth of their income for religious purposes to support clergy and assist the poor. It was payable in money or crops.

In England, tithes were commuted after 1836 for a rent charge which had a basis depending on the price of grain. Tithe Commissioners were appointed and they took another 10 years to dispense with them completely. Many of the Tithe Maps are available in the Record Offices and they make interesting reading, assuming you like history.